GASLIGHTS and GINGERBREAD

GASLIGHTS and GINGERBREAD

Colorado's Historic Homes

by Sandra Dallas

SWALLOW PRESS

Athens Ohio / Chicago / London

A Sage Book of Swallow Press

Copyright © 1965, 1984 by Sandra Dallas
Printed in the United States of America

Revised edition, 1984

Swallow Press books
are published by
Ohio University Press
Athens Ohio 45701

Library of Congress Cataloging in Publication Data

Dallas, Sandra.
  Gaslights and gingerbread.

  Bibliography: p.
  1. Historic buildings--Colorado. 2. Colorado--
History, Local. 3. Architecture, Domestic--Colorado.
4. Colorado--Biography. I. Title.
F777.D3 1984   978.8   83-18208
ISBN 0-8040-0838-8
ISBN 0-8040-0839-6 (pbk.)

To Bob . . . . who else

Contents

Preface to the 1984 Edition   ix
Preface   xi
Acknowledgments   xii

1   Black Hawk • *Lace House*   3
2   Ouray • *Charles Wheeler home*   7
3   Fairplay • *James Marshall Paul home*   11
4   Greeley • *Nathan Meeker home*   15
5   Capitol City • *George S. Lee's Governor's Mansion*   20
6   Leadville • *Healy House*   23
7   Circus-town (Conifer) • *Broken Bar M Ranch*   29
8   Central City • *Gus Center home*   33
9   Steamboat Springs • *James H. Crawford home*   37
10   Fort Collins • *Franklin C. Avery home*   42
11   Idaho Springs • *John Owen home*   47
12   Georgetown • *Maxwell House*   51
13   Aspen • *Luke Short's house*   57
14   Central City • *Billings-Thomas House*   61
15   Salida • *Gray Cottage*   68
16   Breckenridge • *William Forman home*   72
17   Leadville • *George E. King home*   75
18   Trinidad • *Bloom House*   80
19   Aspen • *Pioneer Park*   86
20   Georgetown • *Hamill House*   90
21   Cripple Creek • *Charles N. Miller home*   96
22   Gunnison • *Alonzo Hartman home*   100
23   Montrose • *Thomas B. Townsend home*   107
24   Pueblo • *The Gargoyle House*   110
25   Cripple Creek • *Finn's Folly*   113
26   Tiger-on-the-Swan • *Swan's Nest*   116
27   Silverton • *"Waldheim," Silver Lake Mine*   120
28   Carbondale • *"Brick House" in Roaring Fork Valley*   124
29   Ouray • *Superintendent's house, Camp Bird*   127
30   Redstone • *John Cleveland Osgood's "Cleveholm"*   132
31   Crested Butte • *Jacob Kochevar home*   139
32   Glenwood Springs • *Congressman Edward Taylor's home*   144
33   Antonito • *Frank Warshauer home*   148
34   Boulder • *John McInnes home*   153
35   Sedalia • *Charlford*   158

Bibliography   163

Preface to the 1984 Edition

Eighteen years after *Gaslights and Gingerbread* was written, I set out with some trepidation to retrace the steps of that 1964 literary house tour. The thirty-five stately, whimsical, sometimes tasteless and often fragile relics of Colorado's architectural past included in the book had suffered the ravages of nearly two decades more of use and possibly neglect. How many would I find standing, I wondered, and how many more desecrated under the guise of modernization by unsympathetic owners.

To my delight, I discovered in my 1982 reconnoitering that historic preservation had taken hold across the state. While the Governor's Mansion in Capital city and the Brick House near Carbondale are gone —no great surprise since both were listing badly two decades ago— other candidates for demolition, such as the Lace House in Black Hawk and the Avery House in Fort Collins, have not only survived but have also been restored. The houses in Montrose and Salida, for example, had been listed on the National Register of Historic Places; and even the best maintained houses of 1964—Bloom House in Trinidad and Healy House in Leadville—have been further restored through newly developed preservation techniques.

I should not have been surprised. The first readers of *Gaslights and Gingerbread* often were older people who told me that as children they played in the house in Fort Collins or as teenagers attended balls at the Boulder mansion. For them, the book was a nostalgic trip into a personal past. Today's readers, by contrast, are mostly younger people with no personal knowledge of the houses but a keen interest in Colorado's architectural heritage.

This updated version of *Gaslights and Gingerbread* is written to appeal to both audiences. While the descriptions and stories and folklore of the earlier work are still here, I have included more historical information about the owners and builders.

Except where noted, the photographs are from the original 1965 edition.

Almost as many people helped with this edition as with the original work. I am grateful to old friends and original collaborators, including Mrs. Mumbert Cerise, Mary Ann Chelf, Doris B. Frost, Lulita Crawford Pritchett, and Betty Woodworth. And I owe thanks to a new generation of home owners, researchers, and preservationists: Robert Failing and Father Richard H. Hartmann, Black Hawk; Rudy Harburg, Boulder;

ix

Susan Golder, Breckenridge; Kay Russell and Anne Shultz, Central City; Sharon Bean, Crested Butte; June Newton Bennett, Fort Collins; Ronald J. Neely, Georgetown; Dena Hammar, Glenwood Springs; Catherine Devereux, Greeley; Nancy Manly and Rae Peterson, Leadville; Vicki Van Gemert, Montrose; Doris H. Gregory and Marvin Gregory, Ouray; Carl Jardine, Steamboat; Sylvia Ruland, Redstone; and Ruth Heñritze, Trinidad.

I am deeply indebted to the two superb libraries in Denver—to Eleanor Gehres and the staff of the Western History Department of the Denver Public library: Don Dilley, Bonnie Hardwick, Susan Kotarba, Augie Mastrogiuseppe, Susan Myers, Pam Patrick, Lynn Taylor, and Fred Yonce; and to Maxine Benson, state historian, and the staff at the Colorado Historical Society library: Vicki Diker, Catherine Engel, Glee Georgia, Rachel Homer, Diane Rabson, and Alice Sharp.

My final thanks to Kendal Atchison, who supplied contemporary photographs for this edition, and Harriett Ward, who helped with proofreading.

Preface

Not so many years ago, the main street of Breckenridge was a dapper boulevard lined with jaunty buildings, some of the best gingerbread architecture in Colorado.

Today, most of the structures are gone, and the few remaining have been refaced. Fortunately for history, they were preserved in print and paint by an enthusiastic chronicler, Muriel Sibell Wolle.

The houses that lived with the buildings? Nobody cared much about them, so they lived their exuberant existences and are crumbling away without even the recognition of a picture on a postcard.

These decorative and lavish homes deserve at least a fleeting note in history. *Gaslights and Gingerbread* has been writtten to give them their say.

The book was begun with the idea of including only mountain Victorian homes, and most are just that. But others came along—not really Victorian, nor indeed, even built in the nineteenth century, but unusual enough to merit attention. Despite the title's seeming exclusion, they deserve to be included.

Homes in Denver and Colorado Springs were eliminated since there are enough in each city to fill separate books.

Except when noted, all houses are private residences, not open to the public. Many owners are victims of overly enthusiastic sightseers who punch the doorbell and demand to see inside. So anyone using the book as a tour guide is asked to proceed with courtesy. The owner of one particular interesting home reported coming downstairs dressed in her nightgown early one Sunday morning to find a family peering through the window. They didn't believe anyone "really lived there."

The colonial houses of New England, the mansions of the South, the adobes of California—all have told their tales. Perhaps through *Gaslights and Gingerbread* Colorado's gay and gaudy homes will tell theirs.

Acknowledgments

So many people made this book—those who collected history in memory and manuscript. From the capable women in the Western History Department of the Denver Public Library and the library of the State Historical Society of Colorado, to the efficient Chamber of Commerce secretaries who answered queries and directed letters to local historians.

Space limits the recognition they should have, but though I list them impersonally and thank them collectively, my appreciation is very great.

Perry Eberhart, author of *Guide to the Colorado Ghost Towns and Mining Camps*. William E. Marshall, State Historical Society of Colorado. Mrs. Grace Warshauer McGregor, Antonito. Mrs. Maumbert Cerise, Mrs. Fred Glidden, Vern Harris, Mrs. Harald Pabst, Aspen. Louis Pircher, Mrs. John I. Smith, Black Hawk. Mr. and Mrs. Donald McInnes, Mrs. Julian Peck, Boulder. Mrs. Bertha Biggins, Mrs. Freda Dodge, Amos Jackson, Mrs. Ambure Otterson, Helen Rich, Belle Turnbull, Breckenridge. Mr. and Mrs. Gus Center, Mr. and Mrs. William M. Tanner, Central City. Norman Meyer, Conifer. Bernice Gardner, Fritz Kochevar, Crested Butte. Mrs. William Ackelbein, Mr. and Mrs. George Blaylock, Mrs. Vivian Richardson, Cripple Creek. Mrs. Cathy McKinny, Fairplay. Mrs. Donald Ahrenholtz, Mrs. Alice Stranton, Betty Woodworth, Fort Collins. Torval Johnson, Mrs. Kathryn Senor, Glenwood Springs. Mrs. Richard Bennett, Mr. and Mrs. Hildreth Frost, Jr., Georgetown. Mrs. Helen Larson, Greeley. Mrs. Leah Hartman Cunius, Mrs. Mil Davis, Gene Grubb, Gunnison. Mrs. Frances Cassidy, Idaho Springs. Robert L. Christy, Lamar. Don and Jean Griswold, Emmett Irwin, Mrs. Marion Poppy Smith, Leadville. Osborn R. Lee, Montrose. Mrs. Benton B. Bailey, Mrs. Mabel L. Franz, Mrs. Frances Johnson, Ouray. Mrs. L. J. Farabaugh, Grace Green, Pueblo. Paula Wolfe, Redstone. Mrs. Frank Chelf, Mrs. Harriet Alexander, Salida. Charles Alfred Johnson, Jr., Mrs. Gordon Rogers, Sedalia. Mr. and Mrs. Claude Deering, William A. Way, Silverton. Clay Monson, Margaret and Lulita Pritchett, Ann Rich, Steamboat Springs. Mrs. William S. Iliff, Trinidad.

No work of mine would be complete without my thanks to Daniel B. Moskowitz, Duane Howell, J. Russell Heitman, and most especially Robert T. Atchison, four friends who unknowingly, perhaps, nursed the seeds that grew into this book.

GASLIGHTS and GINGERBREAD

1

Lace House

BLACK HAWK

Weatherbeaten and forlorn, its tattered trim slowly rotting away, Black Hawk's Lace House bore a haunting look of decay, of mountain decadence. For sixty years it sat, lodged against a mountainside, its rotted splendor suggesting the fantasies of a bygone era, until in the 1970s it was restored to its former elegance.

With its whimsical trim, carefully hand-sawed by an unknown carpenter, the Lace House is one of the finest carpenter Gothic houses in the West. But its history is mundane, no match for the elegant house itself.

The house was built in 1863 by Lucien K. Smith, who with his father and uncle built and operated toll roads into Gregory Gulch, the gold rich gully that begins in Black Hawk and extends up the mountain beyond Central City. Smith married, took his wife on a two month honeymoon to Denver, and had the house built while they were away as a surprise for his bride. Smith's cousin, Eben Smith, later prominent in Colorado business, built a similar house up the mountainside on Casey Avenue.

Smith sold the Black Hawk house two years later to Charles Fiske, a local mining man, the first of half a dozen undistinguished purchas-

3

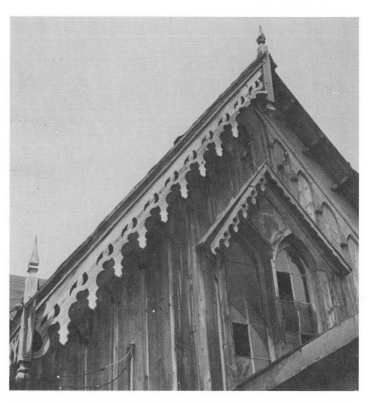

Side gable with chapel window.

ers. In 1896 Rosa Pircher, a widow with four sons, bought the house with insurance money she received after her husband died of "miner's disease"—consumption. When she moved to California after World War I, the house was boarded up and forgotten.

In 1943 the Lace House, by then a weathered relic of the mining boom, was sold to a Greeley schoolteacher, Evelyn Hume, for $10, with the stipulation the buyer repair it. After ignoring countless attempts by vacationers, historians, and preservationists to buy the house, Mrs. Hume deeded the Lace House to Black Hawk in 1974, and the town began its restoration as a Centennial-Bicentennial project.

Some $75,000, part of it federal preservation funds, has been spent restoring the Lace House to its former Victorian elegance. Its location directly across from Nathaniel P. Hill's noisy, smoke-belching smelter kept it from being the most desirable house in the Central City mining district, but the Lace House, named for the elaborate gingerbread carving that drips from the gables and eaves, more than held its own. Not only was its facade eye-catching, but its interior was spacious. There are two front doors. The everyday door, which opens directly into the dining room, was used by family and most visitors, while the "deacon's

Gingerbread trim across the porch.

door" was used only for special occasions, such as when the minister came to call.

The deacon's door opens into the front parlor, and beyond is the small, intimate back parlor. The restored front parlor is papered in rich, swirling, hundred-year-old Victorian paper, purchased in Canada in the 1950s by Robart Failing, a fourth generation Central City resident active in the house's restoration. Failing also provided the house's doorknobs, which he salvaged as a boy from a dilapidated building in Nevadaville, above Central City.

Restored Lace House, 1982.
(Photograph courtesy of Kendal Atchison.)

The dining room has its original pine wainscoting, hand-grained by a workman when the house was built to resemble more expensive wood. Despite years of neglect, the wainscoting required nothing more than soap and water to restore it. Adjacent to the dining room are a scullery and a kitchen, which has been repainted its original two bilious shades of blue. Upstairs are three bedrooms that look out on Black Hawk through chapel-like Gothic windows.

Because federal funds were used in the restoration, Lace House workers were required to save the old square nails from rotted floorboards and use them in the new planks, and to paint the house its original two shades of brown. In addition, the crumbling privy, reached by a long flight of stairs that begin at a second floor door, had to be rebuilt, its vault cleaned out and relimed.

Restoration of the Lace House assures the preservation of an extraordinary example of nineteenth century architectural whimsy; still, it destroys the haunting bit of crumbling splendor that made philosophical passers-by think of the elusive riches of the West's mining towns.

2

Charles Wheeler home

OURAY

Early mining town houses, for the most part, were an ungainly lot, a sort of camp town jigsaw. They usually began as one room log structures, often built with dirt floors and low ceilings. When the need arose or the owner had some leisure time, a second room was added or windows cut in the walls or a second door put in. Sometimes a second story was stuck on top, and if the miner struck a promising vein, he hid the entire place under a coat of siding.

Most of these add-on structures were cumbersome. Occasionally, they were quaint. Only rarely were they charming, and one of these few unusually beautiful homes stands gracefully under the towering cliffs that surround Ouray.

Nobody knows who built the first log cabin on this Oak Street site. Its history really began when the house was purchased by Charles and Abbie Wheeler in 1882 and was gradually expanded over the next fifty years by the Wheeler family until it became a two-story chinked log structure built of thick hand-hewn logs and stained siding. Handsome bay windows and second-floor dormers look out over Ouray. The chimney is red, hand-cast brick, and the inside walls of the house were covered with canvas to keep the chinking from falling into the room. The original cabin was built on a stone foundation, but later parts of the house were constructed directly on the ground. A cookhouse behind the cabin was built from the same squared logs.

Wheeler house on Oak Street after Walter and Abbie Wheeler were married. *(Photograph courtesy Western History Department, Denver Public Library.)*

The cook's cottage.

Wheeler, according to Ouray historian Doris H. Gregory, was one of three brothers who left Massachusetts to settle in Colorado. Charles Wheeler was a surveyor who worked on Otto Mears' treacherous toll road from Ouray to Sneffles. In addition, he was involved in civic water projects and had investments in cattle.

Charles and Abbie Wheeler and their two children lived in their Ouray log house until his death in 1888. Two years later the widow married Walter Wheeler, her husband's nephew and onetime surveying associate. While Abbie was seven years older than her husband, who delighted in shocking acquaintances by telling them: "I married my aunt," the marriage was an unqualified forty-year success. The couple lived in the house for years, later moving to a hotel in Ouray, though the house was not sold until after Abbie's death in 1929.

Walter Wheeler was an enterprising man who dabbled in surveying, mining, and even automobiles, and was once mayor of Ouray. According to Gregory, he once put an advertisement in the *Solid Muldoon,* Ouray's infamous newspaper, for a local opera house:

WANTED! eighteen smooth, symmetrically, even muscled girls for the ballet at Wright's Opera House. Permanent situations. Apply or address giving particulars and dimensions.

Walter F. Wheeler, Ouray, Colorado

Chapel window door with china knob.

Added onto with reason but little intended rhyme, the log cabin on Oak Street nevertheless has a pleasing rhythm today. It is in the shape of two Ls linked together. The front L is chinked log on the first story with stained shingles on the second. Trim on the porch, windows, and the door is green, and there are colorful petunias, orange trumpet vines, and red climbing roses growing over the porch and windows. The back one-story L is covered with wood siding and stained shingles.

Inside, for all its hit-or-miss construction, the house is surprisingly well arranged. There is a living room, dining room, kitchen, and four bedrooms, one of which has been turned into a bathroom. The house has a Shaker appearance with its white-washed canvas walls, which resemble rough plaster more than cloth. The bay windows let in a soft, diffused light.

The fireplace is the one touch of Victorian elegance in all the simplicity. The highly polished carved cherrywood mantle with its mustard colored tile probably was added long after the house was constructed, though, of course, the house was built with a fireplace.

The only primitive sign of the house's humble log cabin beginnings is the low archway from the stairway to the dining room, which probably was the original back door.

Spartan and simple but with a decided charm, Ouray's log house is a happy escape from the ostentatious, sometimes frighteningly gaudy houses of Colorado's mining towns.

Cherrywood fireplace has mustard color tile.

3

James Marshall Paul home

FAIRPLAY

Every western town worth its gold dust has a haunted house. Fairplay's ghost house stands high on a bluff overlooking the town, and it has all the requirements of mystery—rotting exterior, abandoned look, and even an unexplained death.

The house was built in 1873 in the best, or worst, of American Gothic tradition. Big, bulky, high-gabled, disproportionate, it has no handsome mansard or even gay gingerbread. But it is large and commanding, and despite its unkept appearance, the house once was haughty and proud.

James Marshall Paul, a Leadville mining man, built the house for his wife, Laura. She could not adjust to Leadville's high altitude, so her obliging husband built her a home in Fairplay and rode horseback over the 13,000 foot Mosquito Pass to check on his holdings. Paul had come to Colorado during the first years of the gold rush to make his fortune. In 1866 the *Rocky Mountain News* noted: "Our former fellow townsman, J. Marshall Paul, Esq., who is now located at Buckskin, writes us that gulch mining is again looking up in that vicinity."

Despite the glowing report, Paul failed to strike it rich in Buckskin Joe, so he went to Leadville where he was more fortunate. About 1870 he began development of the Printer Boy Mine, which "promises to be one of the richest in the country. We congratulate friend Paul on his good fortune," reported the *News*. Only a few months later the paper called the strike one of the richest lodes in California Gulch and perhaps the entire territory.

As befitted a man who took $9,000 in ore out of a mine in a single month, Paul selected one of Fairplay's high spots for his home. He could see anywhere in town from his hilltop—and everyone could see him. In addition to the huge, disdaining two-story structure, Paul built a stable and a tennis court. The back of the house was built on level land, but the front was on a slope. A long staircase connected the small front porch to a stone embankment and the street below. Later owners covered the embankment with dirt to form a terrace.

In front the house has a two-story bay window with the remnant of a gingerbread rail on top and once-handsome paneling at the bottom. At one time there was a tiny balcony at the second floor window above the front door, but it has rotted away.

The front door opens onto a long hall and narrow staircase. A door to the right leads to the parlor and one farther down to the dining room. The two are connected by a wide archway. Each room has a spacious bay area eight feet high. The ceilings are ten feet. Behind the dining room is the kitchen and to the west a large library, most likely the room where Laura Paul conducted her private school.

The upstairs is a piece of nineteenth century Americana such as that described by Booth Tarkington in *The Magnificent Ambersons:*

> Upstairs were the bedrooms; "mother-and-father's room," the largest; a smaller room for one or two sons, another for one or two daughters; each of these rooms containing a double bed, a "washstand," a "bureau," a wardrobe, a little table, a rocking-chair, and often a chair or two that had been slightly damaged downstairs but not enough to justify either the expense of repair or decisive abandonment in the attic.[1]

Tarkington described the downstairs, too:

> Commonly, the family sat more in the library ... while callers, when they came formally, were kept to the "parlour," a place of formidable polish and discomfort. The upholstery of the library furniture was a little shabby; but the hostile chairs and sofa of the "parlour" always looked new.[2]

Added to this the Pauls probably had lace curtains at the bay windows, gossamer curtains to let in the view of South Park and its majestic mountains sweeping down to the wide plain, but to keep out stares.

Paul used the house as a base for his political and social activities. A member of the territorial council, Paul was active in Republican

---

[1] Booth Tarkington, *The Magnificent Ambersons*. (New York: Grosset & Dunlap, 1918), pp. 7-8.
[2] *Ibid.,* p. 7.

The two-story bay window looks out across South Park.

Most of the gingerbread trim has fallen off and the paneling rotted away.

politics. He was an officer of the International Order of Odd Fellows and a trustee of Wolfe Hall, a Denver school. Governor John L. Routt appointed him to address the Centennial Exposition on the resources of Colorado.

After the Pauls left the house on the hill—Paul died in 1878 and was buried in Philadelphia—it had a series of owners, including one who used the place as a stagecoach stop. Over the years the unkept house was allowed to rot away until now it contains only vestiges of its former grandeur. The exterior, a dull pink, has weathered from lack of paint. The trim long since has fallen off. Years of abuse made the elephantine house too expensive to repair. For some time the old house stood vacant, and it was sold five times for back taxes. Its sad appearance is one reason Fairplay children dub it a haunted house. But there is another.

A number of years ago a young man killed himself in the tiny bedroom at the top of the stairway. Fairplay residents do not reveal anything about the fellow, including the reason for his suicide. But they say the man's parents removed his body, locked the door without cleaning the room, and never entered it again. The next owners painted the floor red to cover the bloodstains.

The house's forbidding look gives credence to the haunted house story, particularly on winter nights when blizzards blow off the mountain range shaking the stark, dark house, rattling the windows and sending out soft, muffled moans.

4

Nathan Meeker home

GREELEY

Journalist Nathan Meeker took seriously the advice of *New York Tribune* editor Horace Greeley, who counseled "Go West, young man." After a trip to the Rocky Mountains where he wrote on irrigation and land development, Meeker, a *Tribune* employee, made up his mind to "go west" permanently.

Meeker was no haphazard wanderer. With the avid enthusiasm of Greeley and the *Tribune,* Meeker organized Union Colony, to purchase land in Colorado for a town and farms. On December 14, 1869, the *Tribune* published "the call" to go west, and hundreds of people flocked to meetings to find out about Meeker's utopian agricultural community. The following spring Meeker and about fifty followers, each of whom had paid five dollars to join the colony and another $150 for land, arrived on the Colorado prairie.

15

The addition to the side, made sometime after the house was built, was removed when the house was turned into a museum. (Photograph courtesy of the Colorado Historical Society.)

Meeker knew how bleak and ugly the site was, though in his enthusiasm he had pictured Colorado as a land of milk and honey. A few of the colonizers, who believed Greeley already was a thriving community, turned around and boarded the next train for the East. The rest glumly moved into makeshift homes. Only Meeker was undaunted. He organized the settlement, laid out the town, and channeled irrigation water for newly planted garden plots. He named the town for his publisher and the streets for trees, planting dozens of fruit and shade trees. Three of them lived. That winter was one of the coldest in Colorado history. The following summer crops were destroyed by grasshoppers. But Meeker persevered.

To show his faith in the fledgling community, he built the finest house in the settlement—far finer than he could afford, in fact—at the corner of Monroe and Plum Streets. Since lumber was scarce, Meeker built the house of adobe blocks, which later were painted yellow. In an 1871 edition of the *Greeley Tribune,* which he edited, he wrote that the blocks "serve better than burned brick, and the walls are not so likely to crack, while they are much cheaper, and the finish may be as good as one can afford."

The Meeker house is square and squat, its plainness relieved only by shutters and an unexpected bit of iron grillework on the roof. The front door is in the center of the house, flanked symmetrically on the first and second floors by windows.

Despite its preeminent position as the finest house in the community, the Meeker home is as no-nonsense inside as outside. The front door opens directly into the parlor. Behind it is the dining room and beyond that, the kitchen. A narrow staircase leads from the dining room to a hallway and three small bedrooms on the second floor.

The Victorian furnishings that Meeker and his wife, Arvilla Delight Smith Meeker, brought to Greeley are in stark contrast to the simplicity of the house. Like other colonists, the Meekers brought fine carved furniture that was thoroughly out of place in the shacks and shanties that served as dwellings for the first few months. Nonetheless, the presence of treasured, familiar belongings helped relieve the despair of Union Colony's hapless pioneer women.

In addition to household necessities, the Meekers brought with them a cherrywood secretary, a parlor set, a diamond dust mirror, a carved black walnut sideboard with marble top, and an assortment of fine china, including tea party dishes that belonged to Josephine, one of the Meekers' four children. Meeker shipped his books while Arvilla brought with her a handsome copy of *The Pilgrim's Progress,* illustrated with colored pictures. The furnishings along with the bric-a-brac that was added later, cluttered up the house and gave it a cramped, cozy Victorian feeling.

Secretary in the front parlor holds books that belonged to the Meeker children.

Meeker acted as shepherd and chief promoter of the Greeley colony until 1878 when he was named Ute Indian agent at the White River Agency on Colorado's Western Slope. Meeker was plagued by debts. From time to time, he had borrowed money from Greeley, who assured Meeker he did not care if it were repaid. But when Greeley died, his estate demanded Meeker make good on the loans. Though Ralph Meeker, the only son, contributed to the family's upkeep from his salary as a New York journalist, and Josephine helped out with her clerical work, Meeker was forced to seek the agency job to repay the loans.

In 1878 Meeker and Arvilla left the Greeley house in care of their daughters Rozene and Mary, took Josephine, and embarked for White River Agency. Meeker was fired with utopian ideas for colonizing the Indians. He envisioned setting up a model farm for the Utes, who would sell their crops to purchase tables and beds and kitchen gadgets, thereby becoming consumers. Greed for the white man's goods, he believed, would encourage them to settle down and prosper as farmers. His policies were a disaster. Only a year after taking the job, Meeker and many of his employees were massacred by Utes, and Arvilla, clutching her copy of *The Pilgrim's Progress,* Josephine, and another woman were taken captive.

The nation's attention was riveted on the plight of the women as speculation centered first on whether they were alive, then whether

This grandfather clock, manufactured in the mid-1880s in Philadelphia, belonged to a Meeker niece.

they had been "outraged," a Victorian euphemism for rape. They had been, but the women coped better than might have been expected. Arvilla took solace in *The Pilgrim's Progress,* which she had snatched up as she was captured, while Josephine actually understood and loved the Utes. She had set up a school for the children, taken their side in disagreements with her father, and she had not altogether believed in his farming policies.

After the women were rescued, they returned to Greeley. Mary Meeker married but died in childbirth in 1883. Josephine moved to Washington and worked as a secretary in the Department of the Interior. She died there in 1882.

Arvilla and Rozene, a queer, bitter woman, whose odd ways were attributed to her having fallen into a well as a child, lived on in the Greeley house. Mrs. Meeker died there in 1905 at the age of ninety, a senile, enfeebled old woman who neglected the house and yard. The house's unkept look and Rozene Meeker's curious ways—she raised chickens, pigs, and other animals in the house—caused rumors about the strange goings on in the old house.

The city of Greeley acquired the Meeker house in 1929 and eventually removed a veranda and addition to the south that had been built after Meeker's death. The house has been restored to its 1870 state and refurbished with the Meeker family's belongings, and today it is a museum. Among the Meeker items displayed are a dress Josephine made out of an annuity blanket during her captivity and Arvilla's prized copy of *The Pilgrim's Progress.*

The kitchen has been refurnished with antiques.

George S. Lee's Governor's Mansion

CAPITOL CITY

George S. Lee was an ambitious man, and he was a dreamer, but he could not seem to make his ambitions and his fantasies work in tandem. His biggest dream as well as his major ambition was to make his city capital of Colorado and himself the governor. In preparation, Lee built the most elegant house in the southern Colorado mining camps to be the governor's mansion. But by the time he finished the home, and most likely even when he began it, Colorado was a state with its headquarters in Denver.

Despite his ambitions, Lee never introduced any legislation to have the state capital moved to the San Juans, and his ambitions did not even get his town the designation of county seat. None of this stopped Lee from changing the town's name from Galena City to Capitol City, however.

But if Lee failed to have his town made into a real capital city, he got some consolation from the fact Capitol City was an important silver mining camp in the San Juans, and he was its leading citizen. He owned a smelter a mile below town, a mill at the other end, and a sawmill in the center, and if he did not own everything else in Capitol City, he at least influenced how it was run.

Inspired by Lee's enthusiasm, local residents planned an overly ambitious city with saloons, stores, hotels, restaurants, smelters, sawmill, post office, numerous homes, and a $1500 school, all for a town that never saw more than 400 residents. Lee's mansion, of course, was the most pretentious building in Capitol City, though a far cry from today's elegant governor's mansion in Denver. Both had conservatories. Lee's house, set in the midst of the majestic San Juans on the bank of rushing Henson Creek, had a more majestic, more inspirational setting. But the Denver mansion edged out the Lee house on the basis of accessibility, space, and indoor plumbing.

The Lee mansion was constructed of brick supposedly mailed to Capitol City since freighting costs were higher than post office charges. The house's conservatory was filled with tropical plants. Large lamps installed on gateposts lit the driveway. The house may even have contained a theater and ballroom. Surrounded by fences and a number of outbuildings including a brick outhouse, the home faced Henson Creek. And Lee always flew a flag from a towering flagpole on top of his residence.

It was inevitable that Lee's home would be the center of Capitol City social life. Frank Fossett in his book, *Colorado,* published in 1880, called the Lee home "the most elegantly furnished house in Southern Colorado," and added: "The handsome brick residence of George S. Lee and lady, distinguished for their hospitality, is a landmark of this locality." The *Lake City Mining Register,* located nine miles away, carried a social item in 1882 about a political celebration held in the Lee house: "The new town officers spread an elegant lunch at Lee's,

Ruins of the governor's mansion.

fascinatingly presided over by Mrs. Lee. Treasurer Lee closed the fes-
tivities with a speech on the future of Capitol City." Lee was not the
only hospitable one. The paper continued: A man named Messler "pro-
nounced the benediction and set 'em up at the Creek."

Another intriguing social event at the Lee mansion was a telephone
concert written up in another Lake City newspaper, *Silver World:*
"Interesting experiment with telephone made last Sunday evening.
Mr. Bates was at the Lake City instruments and Mrs. Lee at those of
her residence in Capitol City. They sang several duets."

The duets did not last for long. The 1893 silver crash destroyed Lee's
dreams of Capitol City as an influential city. After the miners and
saloonkeepers and shop clerks left, the Lees themselves moved away
from Capitol City, leaving their mansion to deteriorate. Scavengers
hauled off the building materials to be used in other structures, and
tourists took bricks as souvenirs, while campers ripped out lumber for
firewood. High winds and the cold helped demolish the fine old place,
and even Henson Creek turned against the house, eating away at the
yard. Today only a few scattered bricks mark the brick building that
was designed to be the most important home in Colorado.

*Fallen timbers and
crumbling walls.*

6

Healy House

LEADVILLE

In 1878 August R. Meyer, one of Leadville's leading residents, married Emma Hixon in the home of two equally upstanding citizens, a storekeeper and his wife, H. A. W. and Augusta Tabor. After the ceremony, Meyer took his bride to the elegant home he had built for her on a Leadville hill, and the couple began what would be a quiet, proper life together—quite unlike that of their wedding hosts, the Tabors.

Meyer, who had studied chemistry and geology in Germany, graduating from the University of Berlin, arrived in Colorado in 1874 and worked for a time as an assayer in Fairplay. He followed the silver boom to Leadville and began construction of his August R. Meyer and Company Ore Milling and Sampling Works in 1876. Meyer generally is credited with bringing successful smelting techniques to the silver camp.

Anxious to marry but dubious about asking a wife to accept the unruly conditions that existed in Leadville, Meyer decided to build his bride an elegant home with every luxury Leadville had to offer, along with a few he freighted in. He designed his imposing green and white two-story house with all the necessities to make a bride happy and the luxuries to make her friends envious. He loved the mountains and chose a site on top of a hill where no building could obscure his view of the Sawatch Range.

The house Meyer built is nostalgically Midwestern with white clapboard siding and green shutters and white picket fence. Its simplicity —by mining town standards, anyway—made it stand out against the decorative, turreted gingerbread houses surrounding it.

Though simple outside, the Meyer home inside was Victorian elegance in its prime. The parlor, by far the finest room in the house, boasted an enormous fireplace painted with fine lines to resemble marble. At first glance it is a fake; at second, a work of art. Because the room, like most parlors, was so seldom used, its exuberantly flowered rug lasted for over a hundred years.

At the top of the narrow staircase, spacious then but nearly claustrophobic now, is a door opening onto a second story porch. There are several bedrooms and (Emma Meyer's friends were justly awed at such a luxury in a mining camp) her own private drawing room. Just above the parlor, the long drawing room runs the length of the house. A beautiful polished fireplace stands along one wall, and the room was furnished with velvet-covered pieces. The paper on the wall is pure Victorian elegance—a deep blue accented with red and black and lavishly covered with gilt designs.

The Meyers lived in their house on the hill only a few years. By then a wealthy man, Meyer sold the house in 1881 to the First Methodist Episcopal Church of Leadville for $4000. The church used the house as a parsonage until selling it in 1886 to Patrick A. Kelly, one time city marshal of Leadville, whose shady dealings had forced him to resign his position.

Mrs. Kelly turned the residence into a fashionable boarding house, carefully selecting her boarders. Several were school teachers, and the 912 Harrison Avenue residence was so popular that Mrs. Kelly moved the stable against the back of the house and rearranged the rooms to accommodate the number of young ladies who applied for rooms.

The house was deeded to Mrs. Kelly's brother, Daniel Healy, in 1888, and he leased it to a couple who continued to rent rooms. At the turn of the century a third story containing four more bedrooms for boarders was added giving the house a gawky, ungainly appearance. In 1912 Nellie A. Healy, a teacher from Michigan who had taught in the Leadville schools for many years, inherited her cousin's house, and in 1936 she gave it to the Leadville Historical Association. Later the house was acquired by the Colorado Historical Society, which runs it as a museum. Tours are given today by guides dressed as 1899 boarders.

A party at Healy House in 1899. *(Photograph courtesy Colorado Historical Society.)*

The weatherbeaten house before it was turned into a museum. *(Photograph courtesy Colorado Historical Society.)*

Second floor drawing room viewed in a diamond dust mirror.

Emblem on the firescreen is one proposed for the Colorado state seal. The fireplace is wood painted to resemble marble, and the wallpaper is a prize-winning French design.

**Dining room chandelier. Wallpaper is
rose, the ceiling a damask-like off-white.**

Healy House has been restored as a stately nineteenth century mansion, an elegant representative of mining camp Victoriana. Today's furnishings, the pick of a number of old homes, are much like the pieces August R. Meyer chose for his bride. In the parlor are a velvet love seat and matching chairs that were hauled to Leadville in a covered wagon from the Atlantic coast. A handsome stained glass triple window fits into the bay window area, and a piano occupies one end of the room.

Across the hall from the parlor, the dining room and smoking room are furnished with heavy Victorian pieces and antique clutter. The kitchen beyond has been refurbished as a turn of the century work room with a scrubbed pine floor and time-saving devices introduced by industrious Victorians.

Throughout the house are lovely pieces of carved black walnut, antique lamps, figurines and dishes, beautiful French dolls, diamond dust mirrors, and even an ornate foldaway bathtub. But by far the most elegant feature of Healy House is its lavish wallpaper, which had been stored away, forgotten, in a warehouse. The paper, bright and gaudy with overbearing patterns, was discovered by the son of a Leadville paper hanger and given to the museum.

The parlor is decorated with a French wallpaper that took first prize at the 1876 Philadelphia Centennial. The paper has a floor-to-ceiling scene of trees, ferns, and flowers. Its border at the top is figured with mountains and mysterious castles. The smoking room and dining room are papered in formal panels with garlanded arches. Even the ceilings are papered much the way they were when August Meyer moved in, with damask-like rich papers. Many of the chandeliers feature elaborate squares at their bases to resemble plaster medallions used on the ceilings of elegant eastern mansions.

Prettiest of all the wallpapers is on the ceiling of a third floor bedroom. At each corner of the ceiling is the likeness of a child with a design of brightly colored flowers and leaves trailing along the walls.

With its combination of old and renovated old, Healy House is a piece of Victoriana revisited.

Ceiling design in a third floor bedroom is a child's head surrounded by brightly colored flowers and leaves.

7

Broken Bar M Ranch

CIRCUS-TOWN

Midway between Denver and Bailey, in a valley gilded in the fall with shimmering leaves of burnished aspen, stands a stately yellow farmhouse with rose-colored shutters. Deceptively genteel, the house looks like a midwestern farmhouse, but the history of the Broken Bar M Ranch, as it is called today, is as gaudy as the house itself.

Marauding Indians terrified early settlers. Local legend tells that after one party of Indians ravaged the valley, burning and plundering, an Indian brave forced a settler to sew a button onto his shirt just a few inches from where two fresh scalps dangled from his belt. Even stranger were the elephants that once roamed the valley munching mountain meadow grass. P. T. Barnum, who had financial interests in Denver, chose the ranch as a winter watering spot for his elephants and other circus animals. Barnum's workers dubbed the site "Circus-town."

The land was homesteaded in the 1860s by Duncan McIntyre, a former British seaman. As a member of Her Majesty's Navy, McIntyre protested the flogging of a shipmate, struck the punishing officer, and was thrown into irons. When his ship docked in Montreal, he deserted and roamed the far north as an employee of Hudson's Bay Company for several years until Queen Victoria pardoned deserters. McIntyre

Window above the front doors is filled with colored glass.

returned to civilization—a homestead in Colorado filled with Indians, wild animals, and elephants. He erected a barn, which still stands, made of timbers held together with wooden pegs, a sod house, and fashioned a pipeline made of hollowed-out logs to bring water from a spring to his house. Perhaps McIntyre found the combination of Indians and elephants too much for him because he gave up the ranch in the 1880s and moved away.

The second owner, Louis Ramboz, commissioned the big midwestern farmhouse in 1889. Ramboz, a Frenchman, came to Colorado in 1859 and engaged in farming. Shortly afterward he married Holymphia LeFiever, in Saint Joseph, Missouri, and brought her west. She died not long before Ramboz built the house.

In 1950 when owners were installing a heating system, they discovered a board nailed to a joist under the landing of the staircase with a penciled history of the house.

Original wallpaper in the front hall in shades of brown with gilt.

Circus-town, October 1889. This house is been built by Joseph Grauffel of the city of Denver for Mr. Louis Ramboz is been commenced in March 1889 and finished in October the same year.

Joseph Grauffel, contractor builder

Ramboz designed a large house of twelve rooms, six on each floor. The front had a comfortable porch and handsome double doors with a window filled with colored glass panes above them. There was a decorative gingerbread widow's walk on the roof around the chimney, which has been replaced with iron grillework, a weather vane, and lightning rods. The building, which was constructed without running water, wiring, or central heating, cost $2,500.

The foyer, the only portion of the house with its original decor, has a well-kept staircase zig-zagging across one wall. The paper, only slightly shredded, has been carefully preserved. The pattern is a geometric design in mountain colors—gold, rust, brown, and yellow—embellished with gilt.

Ramboz liked fancy doors, which are the most attractive feature inside the house. Most of them have china knobs, but the front door knob is brass with daisy designs cast into it. Hinges and locks are patterned metal, too. And the doors are handgrained. Some seem as if their varnish was combed just before it dried while the deep rust stain on others appears like a child's finger painting.

While Louis Ramboz owned the home, it was used as a boarding house as well as a stage stop for passengers who could not find room in the inn a few miles farther on. At times the house was so crowded

Brass front-door knob was cast with a daisy design.

that some visitors had to sleep in the barn. Local legend tells that two women arrived in the midst of a winter storm seeking a place to stay, and the next morning found themselves snowbound. They stayed for a week, and when they asked for a bill, their hosts refused to give them one saying the women had livened up a dreary winter week. The two women, the story goes, were Helen Hunt Jackson, author of *Ramona,* and an artist friend, and several weeks later they sent their hosts an excellent oil painting. Jackson, however, died in 1885, before the house was built. Still, for years a fine oil painting, sent by two women guests, hung over the fireplace at Circus-town.

In 1913 the house was sold to a Scotsman, R. W. Kirkpatrick, for $11,000. The price included the furnished home and land, farming equipment, and livestock. The new owner shipped the first automobile to the valley, renting an entire freight car to house the vehicle in solitude on its journey from Oregon to Denver.

Kirkpatrick brought another change to the Circus-town valley. He erected the first fences. To protect himself from open range advocates, Kirkpatrick carried a gun while he dug the postholes though he placed the posts twenty-five feet inside his property line to minimize arguments. Later, placement of the fences caused problems when adjacent land was subdivided.

In 1950 the house was purchased by Norman F. Meyer, a Continental Airlines pilot, and named the Broken Bar M Ranch. Meyer whittled it down in size from Kirkpatrick's 1,200 acres to a mere 500 and completely remodeled the farmhouse. The Meyer family painted the weathered residence its bright yellow and added rose-colored shutters. They refurbished the grillework and took off part of the porch, eliminated doors and cut new windows.

Inside, the entrance hall was left alone, but other rooms were rearranged and central heating and plumbing added. The house was built without fireplaces so the new owners installed three.

They redecorated and refinished, but despite the changes, the house retains its farmhouse ambience. And the Meyers, like the original builder, Louis Ramboz, have preserved their own portion of the Circus-town story. When they built one fireplace, they wrote down their part in the house's history and sealed it behind the stones, perhaps to be found years from now by some distant owner.

8

Gus Center home

CENTRAL CITY

High up on Central City's Eureka Street stood an undistinguished, misshapen little house of little architectural merit. It was built in the 1870s or 1880s by Hans Jacob Kruse, a German immigrant who arrived in Central in 1860 to find gold but instead became a baker. Twice mayor of Central City, Kruse was in office during Central City's disastrous 1874 fire. Later the home was acquired by George McFarlane, a member of another pioneer family.

But the house's real history began in 1944 when Gus and Verdi Center purchased it and recreated one of the state's most exuberant Victorian dwellings, unabashedly combining the best and worst of nineteenth century America into a charming example of mountain Victoriana.

First the Centers rebuilt the house, turning windows around, pulling out doors, adding a lawn in front and a grotto in back. An old photograph shows the house a washed out color, probably white, with dark trim. The Centers changed the color to Victorian rose with red trim and black iron accents.

Walls as well as ceilings were covered with the best copies of mid-Victorian wallpaper available. A fancy iron coal stove was added to the living room, and an iron and porcelain cook stove was installed in the kitchen, its burners wired for electricity.

"This house belongs to everybody because everybody has made it what it is," said Mrs. Center. "Anything that anybody didn't want came here." Some of the furnishings are family heirlooms such as Cousin Perry's copy of *The Pilgrim's Progress,* printed around 1880. Others are gifts from friends. The handsome kerosene lamp hanging in the kitchen came from Mr. and Mrs. William Tanner, who owned the Gothic revival house farther down Eureka Street. Many furnishings were purchased by the Centers, who were indomitable collectors.

The front door of the house opens directly into the little parlor, which is neat and tidy. The ingrain carpet on the floor is more than 100 years old though barely worn. Delicate lace curtains are held in place by mercury-luster tiebacks. The upright piano, covered with a fringed throw, is an heirloom. Mrs. Center's father, Lincoln Markham, gave the instrument to his wife when their first daughter was born. Its top is covered with Victorian mementos, and the three books kept there— a collection of Elizabeth Barrett Browning's poems, a Methodist hymnal, and a Bible full of family clippings—were on the piano when Mrs. Center was a little girl.

The parlor is a reproduction of a nineteenth-century sitting room.

Scarlet lamp came from a Central City brothel.

Victorian kitchen clutter.

The only original furnishings still in the house are the love seat and matching chairs in the parlor. Above them is a charming American primitive of a curly-haired girl with Renoir eyes who is twisting a moonflower vine through her fingers.

The tiny library off the parlor has a small melodeon, and hanging over it is a picture of Mrs. Center's grandfather. The bookshelves are filled with leather-bound volumes, including an 1804 edition of *A Lady's Advice to Her Children.* Along one wall is the couch on which Lincoln Markham courted his wife.

The dining room would have won the heart of any Victorian lady, especially the women of the gold towns who left their lovely things behind them and came fortune hunting with only the ugliest and most utilitarian equipment. There are treasured silver teapots, sugarbowls and creamers, salt dishes, a fruit stand, and spoon holders. The table is covered with a chenille between-meal cloth, which was removed and replaced by a regular tablecloth for meals. A beautifully carved black walnut buffet with marble top, a fainting couch, and a sewing box with beaded pincushion in the shape of a high top shoe are in the room.

In addition, there are *Godey's Lady's Book* prints, watercolors by an aunt, oils by another relative, and pastels by Mrs. Center's mother. In front of the window, framed by lace curtains held with Tiffany tiebacks, is the height of Victorian luxury—a scarlet "Gone with the Wind" lamp. This one came from an early Central City brothel.

Up a flight of precipitously steep stairs decorated with old prints including one by Charles Dana Gibson, are two bedrooms. Though all too many Victorian sleeping rooms were decorated with leftovers, these are furnished with handsome bedroom pieces, including spool beds and marble-topped walnut dressers.

There is a child's rocker and a family rocking chair in which a favorite aunt rocked her babies. Lincoln Markham's Masonic papers are preserved, as well as a decorative marriage certificate lettered in Spencerian tracery, two handworked pillow covers embroidered with "A Glorious Morning Unto You" and "Go to Sleep Like the Flowers."

Victorian women were proud of their handiwork, which was cherished and affectionately given to friends. One of the nicest customs of the nineteenth century was the friendship quilt. These handsome spreads were made for neighbors in distress, for families moving West, sometimes to honor a minister or teacher or hero, or for a betrothed girl. Each woman embroidered a block, then the group met to "set" the top and do the "putting in."

Sometimes young women made quilts for men they liked, and Lincoln Markham's women friends embroidered one for him. The Markham quilt is especially handsome, a crazy quilt made with brilliantly colored scraps of silk and velvet held together with a hundred different delicate, feathery stitches. Each woman pieced a square, embroidered it with her initials, and sometimes embellished it with ribbon or chenille flowers, the date (1884) or special little designs.

Like the coverlet, the Center home on Eureka Street is a crazy quilt of brilliant pieces of Victoriana pieced together with unabashed enthusiasm.

Lincoln Markham's friendship quilt.

James H. Crawford home

STEAMBOAT SPRINGS

American tradition insists the West was settled not by greedy, grubbing fortune seekers, as it often was, but by honest, brave pioneers, who sacrificed the comforts of civilization to turn the wilderness into a home. Margaret and James H. Crawford were just such pioneers. If they left civilization behind in Missouri, they took with them the principles of self-sacrifice and hard work and a sense of hospitality and friendliness.

The Crawfords with their three children settled first in Hot Sulphur Springs in 1874. During much of their first long winter, Crawford lived in a cave tending his cattle while Maggie Crawford cared for the children as well as various kinfolk and guests in a log cabin in town. A local saloonkeeper, who left to spend the winter months in more comfortable surroundings, left his store of brandy with Maggie Crawford, the only person in the camp he could trust not to drink it.

Before the winter set in, Crawford wandered through western Colorado searching for a site suitable for a ranch and found it near a place

Colored glass panes in the front door.

Paneled staircase in the entrance hall.

the Utes called Medicine Springs. One spring made such a distinctive chugging sound that Crawford named the site Steamboat Springs. That fall Crawford built a rock foundation and put up a claim notice to hold the land. The following year he began the walls, and eventually the chinked log cabin emerged as four rooms built in the shape of a cross around a central court. The story of the Crawford cabin is told by granddaughter Lulita Crawford Pritchett in *The Cabin at Medicine Springs.*

Later the Crawford family erected a white frame house in Steamboat Springs, and in the 1890s, they built a fine stone house on top of Crawford Hill.

By then Crawford, as the founder of Steamboat Springs, was a successful rancher and civic leader. He had been named Steamboat postmaster by Governor Routt after complaining about the distance he had to travel to pick up the mail. Crawford personally made a trip to ask for better service from the governor, and when he returned home, he found a mail sack containing a few supplies and his commission as postmaster.

Like the other Crawford houses at Steamboat, the mansion at Medicine Springs was a warm, friendly place, open to all travellers. Visiting dignitaries were enthusiastically entertained, but so was old Frank Ding, a trapper.

The three-story home was constructed of native stone quarried on Woodchuck Hill, a quarter of a mile west of the house, and hauled to the building site by teams of animals. The stonework was done by a stonemason named Briggs, who worked in Steamboat only a short time. The Crawfords, it seemed, were the only people who could afford a stone house. Crawford, himself, oversaw the construction and said he handled every stone that went into the house.

The Crawford mansion is a large square structure. The front door is set in a large stone archway that Crawford loved. On either side of the door is a narrow window set with panes of colored glass—blue, gold, and opaque white as well as a red and white star-like design. The wide front porch was added later.

The entrance hall is spacious and friendly, big enough for guests to mingle comfortably as they took off their coats or bundled up for the sleigh ride home on cold nights. Along one wall is a handsomely paneled staircase with a built-in seat. Across from the stairs are a fireplace and bookshelves. But by far the most memorable object in the hall was the immense deer head with its enormous antlers, a record spread, over the mantel. Crawford liked to tell spellbound guests how he and his greyhound, Legs, had cornered the animal, and he had shot it with a Colt .44.

The living room has a pretty cherrywood fireplace. In the evenings, the Crawfords and their friends liked to sit around the fire and sing or listen to tales of early day Steamboat. Next to it, the dining room is big enough to seat many people, which it often did, and the built-in cupboard is large enough to hold a good-size china service with enough pieces to serve a long table of guests.

The kitchen is another large, cheery room, and guests gathered there, too, to chat while Maggie Crawford fried young sage chicken or prepared strawberry shortcake, much as the Indian women had gathered to gossip in the log cabin while Mrs. Crawford poured molasses over biscuits for them.

On the second floor are four bedrooms, and curving up from the master bedroom to the third floor is a pretty staircase, paneled in tongue-in-groove siding. Guests who panted up the stairs were warned not to knock their heads on the massive mountain sheep horns beside the third floor door or trip over the prongs of the elk horn chair. The third floor was the Crawford den where the family kept Indian relics, guns, grizzly, fox, and wolverine pelts, and a mounted mountain lion. Besides acting as a museum, the third floor served as a lookout station. Whenever the fire siren blew, one of the Crawfords ran to the third floor window to spot the fire and tell the others its location.

Since the cabin days, the Crawfords had been known for their hospitality. Anyone passing through Steamboat Springs was welcome at the Crawford house, and at times there were beds made up all over the house. At night Crawford liked to turn on all the lights in the house

The Crawford residence in the early 1900s (Photograph courtesy Lulita Crawford Pritchett.)

so that every window blazed forth hospitality. But along with serving as a way station for travellers, the Crawford home was the social center of Steamboat society. Literary guilds, socials, and discussion groups were held in the house along with musicales since the Crawfords owned the first organ in town. While the grownups chatted inside, the children braided chains of pink and white clover that grew in the yard or hunted for eggs and kittens in the spacious barn.

The house at the top of Crawford Hill was a happy place, and the Crawfords were good, generous people. Crawford would have died a much wealthier man if he had not been so open-handed. Said one loyal Crawford friend when asked if anything scandalous ever took place in the Crawford home: "Lord! If it was the Crawfords, there wouldn't have been a scandal!"

Perhaps the most memorable event the big stone house ever knew was the golden wedding anniversary party for James and Margaret Crawford, May 25, 1915. Friends came from all over northwestern Colorado to pay tribute to the couple who in pioneer days had weathered many hardships but who through the years never had failed to befriend travellers up and down the valley.

10

Franklin C. Avery home

FORT COLLINS

Franklin C. Avery was one of the ambitious young visionaries who answered New York publisher Horace Greeley's call to go west to settle the land. With some fifty other pioneers, young Avery, who was barely twenty-one years old, joined Nathan Meeker's Union Colony, which settled Greeley in 1870. As a civil engineer, he helped Meeker survey the townsite and lay out its streets.

Shortly afterward a group of Greeley settlers formed a second agricultural colony to settle Fort Collins, thirty miles away. Avery was a member of the new colony, and once again he surveyed and laid out the new town. Asked why he planned such wide streets in both Greeley and Fort Collins, Avery replied: "People need wide streets, and land's cheap, so I give 'em to them."

In 1876 Avery returned to New York to marry Sara Edson, whom he had courted by letter, and not long after they set up housekeeping in Fort Collins, Avery began construction of his handsome home on Mountain Avenue. The sandstone keystone over the front door is carved with the completion date, 1879.

Avery prospered in Fort Collins, and his fine home reflected his success. He built the Avery Block, which contained a bank, several stores, and office space. He was elected county surveyor, served on the town council, and had a financial interest in the opera house and the Northern Hotel. And in 1882, three years after the house was completed, Avery founded the First National Bank, serving as its president until his retirement in 1910.

It was only natural that a man as prominent as Avery with an auspicious career before him would build an imposing house. The Avery house was not only imposing, however. It was capricious. The Avery house has the whimsical look of a fairy tale cottage.

Constructed of native stone quarried at nearby Bellvue and decorated with red sandstone, the Avery house has a large central gable in front. The roof is accented with numerous dormer windows, irregular corners, and crevices. The corners of the house and the windows are etched with dark sandstone. Trim is painted a loden green while a tiny red wooden border outlines the glass in the windows.

The evergreen trees surrounding the house, planted by Avery and grown to massive size now, add to the storybook look. So do the tipped-up edges of the roof, the pretty birdbath made of sandstone that matches the house, the rustic stone porch posts, and the gabled stable (which is a house now). In the side yard there is a trim little gazebo with a rustic roof which the Averys used for church ice cream socials.

The house and its 1893 addition, so cleverly married to the original that it is difficult to tell the two apart, cost Avery a total of $7,000.

If the Avery house has the appearance of a Hansel and Gretel cottage, the inside is conventional Victorian. The front hall, a large room which runs nearly two-thirds of the front of the house, has a prominent and beautifully carved oak staircase. Avery, who designed the house, specified that both outside and inside walls were to be a foot thick, so the window sills are wide enough for window seats.

The year when the house was completed is on the keystone over the front entrance.

Picnics and socials were held in the gazebo in the side yard.

Avery home about the turn of the century *(Photograph courtesy of Poudre Landmarks Foundation.)*

*Curled brass fixture in
the dining room had
delicate yellow shades.*

A wide archway, decorated with pillars at each side and an oak pediment at the top, separates the hall and dining room with its built-in china cupboard. The fine brass gaslight fixture in the dining room, which has disappeared, had two pretty buttercup-shaped globes of yellow overlay glass. Next to the dining room is the kitchen with waist-high wainscoting, and behind it a room for the hired girl.

Like any really good Victorian house, the Avery home has both a front and a back parlor, and these are larger than most. Avery, it seems, liked the rooms in his house to be as spacious as the streets he laid out surrounding it. The front parlor has a marble-inlaid, carved cherry fireplace. The marble, a veined black, has insets of streaked white marble. The room was furnished with cherry pieces from New York. The tower on the east side of the house forms an attractive windowed alcove in the back parlor that is neatly fitted with a curved radiator.

There are five bedrooms upstairs, complicated, strangely shaped rooms fitted under the eaves. Though the Averys had only three children who survived childhood, the rooms could accommodate a good many more people and usually did since elderly relatives often lived with the family. One of them was Mrs. Avery's Aunt Philomena Edson, who spent her time weaving blankets. Another aging relative, Mrs. Avery's mother, Elizabeth Edson, rued the day she came west and spent her time at the depot wistfully watching the trains depart.

The master bedroom is a double room with a round alcove above the back parlor. It has a private bathroom. Another bedroom, a double room, zigzags in and out under the roof and dormer windows, while a third has a sun porch and two tiny auxiliary rooms.

The Avery house was an active place. There was a cave in the back yard and a tree house, and picnics were set up near the gazebo. Shetland ponies and the Averys' Saint Bernard dog pranced in the yard among the fruit trees. For special occasions the yard was decorated with Chinese lanterns, and bands played in the gazebo.

But the Averys' life was not all picnic suppers and brass bands. In 1890, Avery's brother died, and his widow was put on trial for murder, though she was eventually acquitted. Later the Averys' son-in-law, a lawyer, was shot and killed by a client.

Franklin and Sara Avery lived in the home until 1917 when they moved to California for his health. Family members continued to live in the house for nearly fifty years, until it was sold in 1962. For a dozen years the future of the Avery house, located adjacent to Fort Collins' expanding downtown district, looked bleak. Then in 1974 the city purchased the house for $79,000. Today, under the auspices of the Poudre Landmarks Foundation, the Avery house, through state and federal funds, local business grants, and even girl scout donations, is being restored to its enticing fairy tale splendor.

John Owen home

IDAHO SPRINGS

Like many of his Confederate compatriots, John Owen came west after the Civil War to rebuild his shattered life. Born into a family of southern planters, Owen, a Confederate soldier, was captured eleven times by Yankees and escaped ten times.

At the war's end, he opened a mercantile store, but it failed, and hearing tales of silver strikes in Leadville, Owen headed west to work in the mines. He made $2,000 in little over a year and sent for his wife and young son and daughter to come to Idaho Springs.

As a mining operator and speculator, Owen was known for his honesty, according to a contemporary biography, which was probably underwritten by Owen. He invested in the Gum Tree Mine, the Dove's Nest, the Sun and Moon, the Blue Bird, and the Red Elephant, all in the Idaho Springs area. And if he was honest and sometimes generous —he claimed the Gum Tree paid the highest wages of any mine in the vicinity—he also was shrewd. Owen combined his southern manners with Yankee practicality to pull off a neat political maneuver to determine the outcome of a Clear Creek County election.

As a Southerner, Owen was, of course, a Democrat, but most of his miners were Republicans, and several hundred miners could swing any

47

Glass-studded, gilded light fixture in the hall.

Parlor with tile-inlaid mahogany fireplace.

election in the county. So on election day Owen, as a stalwart if once rebellious member of the Republic, told his miners he would give them time off to go to the polls to vote. But, he added, any man who worked all day would get double pay. Owen knew his miners. Patriotic though they were, they were even more mercenary, and legend says not a single one left his job to vote. The Democrats won the election.

Like the man, the house Owen bought in Idaho Springs was Yankee practicality with Southern embellishments. The architecture is mining camp Victorian—a big, rambling house with gingerbread trim—but there are wide porches in front on both the first and second stories, just big enough to be called verandas by a nostalgic southerner. And inside was an organized maze of Victorian trappings, room after room filled with solid mahogany furniture shipped from Mississippi.

The Owen house, high up on Virginia Street on the side of a mountain, was originally grey clapboard that later was painted white and green. The stable behind it that once housed the Owen horses and carriages has been turned into a second residence. The Owen home, which is plainer than many of the Idaho Springs ornate Victorians, has an air of dignity. There is a latticework fence and fancy brackets at the top of the porch columns. The vertical decorations under the gables look like dagger sheaths in relief. The windows have just the quirk-of-an-eyebrow tilt at the top, and the veranda balustrades look like hand-in-hand cut-out paper dolls.

Like many Victorian houses, the Owen home opens onto a long narrow hall with a staircase hugging one side. It is lit by an elegant gilded globe studded with large chunks of jewel-like colored glass and could be pulled up and down so one could light the candle inside. A second candle fitted into a hole in the top of the newel post, and the candles cast flickering shadows on the German cuckoo clock that performed in the hallway for nearly 100 years and on the stairway carpet made by Mary Owen, John Owen's daughter.

To the west of the hall is the parlor with a tile-inlaid, coal burning fireplace with mahogany frame. Near it were a mahogany settee and chairs brought from Mississippi and decorated with needlework pillows made by Mrs. Owen and the dutiful Mary, who once was described as "a zealous member of the Episcopal Church." The original wallpaper was a spider-like design that wound its way up one wall, across the ceiling, and down another wall. The rug with its massive garlands of bright flowers completed the webby enclosure. A curled brass gaslight fixture hung from the ceiling.

Through a spindlework archway elaborately draped with rich, dark damask silk, the dining room was furnished with the same Southern mahogany furniture. Mrs. Owen kept her fragile green and white Haviland tea set in an antique buffet. Also displayed in the buffet were pieces of china handpainted by Mary Owen, who combined that art with needlework and prayer.

Adjacent to the dining room is a warm, cozy sitting room with another elaborately carved archway to the bay window alcove. Despite its sunny atmosphere, the room was decorated with dark wallpaper, probably a royal blue with a tiny flower design. At the back of the house is the kitchen as well as a bedroom and a bathroom which the Owen family claimed was the first indoor bathroom in Idaho Springs. Its tin tub was painted, and the Owen granddaughter remembered whenever she took a bath in it, the paint came off in little flakes and stuck to her skin.

Upstairs are three bedrooms and a second bathroom, which was added sometime after the Owens moved into the house. The bedrooms were filled with good Southern furniture—high bedsteads, mahogany bureaus, and rocking chairs. There was even a tufted leather fainting couch in the master bedroom.

As befitted their southern background, the Owens were gracious, hospitable people, and over the years they entertained a number of guests. Once Owen went east to interest potential investors in his Clear Creek mining properties and returned with a likely prospect who wanted to inspect the property personally. He visited Idaho Springs as Owen's houseguest and slept in the upstairs front bedroom. The visitor, Henry Ford, apparently liked what he saw because he invested in the mine.

Another guest who spent a summer in the Owen home, sleeping in the same guest room, was Mrs. Owen's pretty first cousin, Edith Bolling Galt, who later became President Woodrow Wilson's second wife.

The Owens lived out their lives in their Idaho Springs home. She died in 1928, and he lived only three years longer. Their daughter Mary inherited the house and lived in it until her death in 1961 when her daughter, Frances Cassidy inherited it. Mrs. Cassidy lived on in the house, which had been updated and relieved of some of its heavy trappings but retained the same mahogany furniture, the needlework pillows, and the handmade carpet, until her death. In 1971, after nearly 100 years in the Owen family, the big southern house was sold.

Elaborate archway between the parlor and dining room.

12

Maxwell House*

GEORGETOWN

Grubstaking was a slightly more reliable way of finding gold or silver mines than daydreaming. No self-respecting gambler would have taken grubstake odds, but a few soft touch storekeepers thought the odds just good enough to loan a prospector that small but highly important stake —his grub (and occasionally his prospecting equipment)—for part interest in anything the miner found.

One lucky grubstaker was H. A. W. Tabor, who parlayed a few dollars worth of food into a Leadville silver strike worth millions. Another fortunate storekeeper was Georgetown grocer Virgil B. Potter, who staked himself into part interest in the productive Colorado Central Mine.

*One of the ten outstanding examples of Victorian architecture in the United States.

When Potter struck it rich, he was living high up on the hill above Georgetown in a crowded one-story little house built in 1867. With his new wealth, he decided that such a simple, unpretentious house was not nearly grand enough for a mining magnate, so in 1889 he built a $35,000 addition in front that was so spectacular it made the rear of the house as dull as servants' quarters.

Like many of the elegant homes of that time, the remodeled Potter house was copied from a magazine. Victorian architects often designed houses and sold plans to journals where they were copied by less imaginative builders and tailored to homeowners' tastes. A detail might be added or subtracted, the porch lengthened, the parlor pinched in.

The house could be as simple or as elegant as the owner wished, and Potter wished it to be very elaborate—so elaborate, in fact, that his home was chosen by an American Institute of Architects' publication of the 1930s as one of the ten outstanding examples of Victorian architecture in the country.

When the silver crash came in 1893, Potter lost his fortune and sold his fine home to Frank A. Maxwell, who lived in it for more than forty-five years. When Maxwell died in 1939, his funeral services were held in the house.

Maxwell was a competent mining engineer, but his fame came from the spectacular Georgetown Loop, which as assistant engineer, he helped design. Part of a Union Pacific branch line, the remarkable loop was a twist of rail and trestle that allowed a train to circle around, gathering momentum to travel from Georgetown to Silver Plume, only two miles away but 600 feet higher.

During the half-century he lived in Maxwell House, Frank Maxwell added a second story addition in the rear but made few other changes, one reason why the home has kept its Victorian appearance. Another is that the present owners, keenly aware of Maxwell House's historical and architectural importance, have studied old photographs and talked with Georgetown old-timers about the house's appearance and decorated it just the way it was originally. Even during the 1950s and 1960s when Alpine chalets and modern cottages invaded Georgetown, Maxwell House stood staunchly Victorian.

Painted pink, brown, coffee, and off-white, Maxwell House with its jaunty cupola and spire is a happy blend of ostentation and practicality. It combines the architectural features of several countries. The windows are Italian, the mansard roof French, and the spire, pure "lighting rod" Americana.

There is a pretty little stoop with railing and pillars and on its roof, a balcony decorated with a sunburst in its paneling. The balcony, of course, is decoration; no door opens onto it. The cupola with its own private mansard roof has a dormer window poking out each side and is topped with a spire that looks like a lightning rod rendered in wood.

Stained glass windows surround the front door.

Parlor door painted to resemble oak.

Gaslight fixture with Sandwich glass globes.

Fireplace shell in the parlor.

The Italian windows in the front of the house protrude slightly; the bottom one is decorated with pillars in relief. Under the cornice are square designs that stand out like the teeth of a happy gap-tooth grin. The mansard on the sides of Maxwell house is roofed with rows of wooden shingles cut in scalloped and pointed designs.

The glass panels above and to the sides of the front door, like the glass at the top of the parlor window, are encrusted with jewel-colored flowers of leaded glass, miraculously unbroken after all these years. The handsome flowers with their diamond-like centers are pink, pastel blue, green, and amber.

Like many houses of the time, Maxwell House opens onto a long hallway with a staircase hugging one wall. It is lit with the soft pink glow from an acorn squash-shape fixture of cranberry colored Sandwich glass overlaid with milk glass.

To the left of the entrance is the parlor with its handgrained door. Victorians often used cheap wood for doors and woodwork and then painted the grain of a finer wood on them. This one is grained to resemble oak.

Still furnished with the original furniture, the parlor is formal but only slightly stiff. Along one wall is a highly polished fireplace, or at least the shell of one. There is no working fireplace, only a chimney pipe. A practical Franklin stove was placed in front of the fireplace mantel since stoves were more efficient and more comfortable than open fires. High up on the walls is the original molding, and hanging from the ceiling is an old gaslight fixture with its morning-glory globes of pastel Sandwich glass.

Beyond the parlor is a study, complete with original fainting couch, and beyond that is the dining room, large and spacious with a huge table. Maxwell kept his collection of rock specimens in this room since after supper talk normally turned to mining, and it was easy to reach over to the shelf, grab a rock, and say: "Now this piece . . ." Maxwell's collection of rocks is still kept in the dining room along with rock specimens of present owners, a prominent Colorado engineering family.

Behind the dining room is a kitchen, which has been modernized. This room probably was the Potter parlor during the grocery days. There is a breakfast room and a bathroom, originally a bedroom, — both part of the old house.

The double back porch dates to the mining days. No matter how prominent Maxwell was, he was relegated to the position of any Georgetown worker when he came home. He was ordered to shed his dirty clothes on the first porch and don clean ones on the second. Still sitting on the porch is the carpeted bench Maxwell sat on to take off his shoes.

Upstairs are the master bedroom and two smaller bedrooms, all added during the Potter refurbishing. Maxwell added two bedrooms of his own. The master bedroom is an elegant suite with a small sitting room and bedroom stretching across the front of the house. In one corner is a pretty little alcove formed by three windows and the mansard roof. There are two staircases in the house and a bath with a big zinc-coated copper tub. Potter probably added the bathroom.

Battered by the winds of a century, Maxwell House is remarkably well preserved. It stands overlooking Georgetown, a remnant of a pretentious era, a monument to a gamble that paid off.

Master bedroom alcove is formed by dormer window in the mansard roof.

13

Luke Short's house

ASPEN

More desperadoes bit the dust in a snappy, seemingly innocent little house on a shady Aspen street than ever were gunned down on the town's streets during Aspen's wild past. These infamous men came from the pen of Luke Short, author of *Blood on the Moon, Ramrod, Silver Rock, Ride the Man Down,* and *Fiddlefoot,* owner of the house, who wrote two-thirds of his fifty brawling westerns while living there. Though Short's office was in downtown Aspen, on summer days he sometimes wrote in the shade of the side yard, just beyond the old white up-and-down picket fence.

One of the prettiest gingerbread houses in Aspen and certainly the most coquettish, the Glidden home (Luke Short was the pseudonym of Frederick Glidden) was an unlikely place for such adventures as Short turned out. No den of double-dealing badmen or haunt of fast-talking fancy women, the house has a happy, carefree air with its proper white and grey siding trimmed with shiny black doors and lace curtains.

Common Aspen front porch decor: skis.

During Aspen's Victorian years the house, in fact, was known for its brilliant parties.

The quaint home was built about 1882 by a druggist, David Mulford Van Hoevenbergh, a New Yorker who began his Aspen career as a cashier in the Jerome B. Wheeler Bank on the first floor of the Wheeler Opera House. Van Hoevenbergh later went into mining, and in 1887 he was listed as treasurer of the Compromise Company, which owned mining properties in the Aspen mining district.

Van Hoevenbergh did not own the house long. Shortly after he built the home it was sold to a mine manager named Heatherly, then to a series of owners until world famous skiing figure Friedl Pfeifer purchased it. Pfeifer sold it to Mr. and Mrs. Glidden in 1948. Glidden died in 1975 and his wife several years later.

The house is a mansard topped with a fancy black iron "catwalk" around the roof; the Gliddens said the area was too small for a widow's walk. Vertical supports in the grillework, each topped with a star, match vertical seams in the roof. The prim little house was well built and even had insulation for Aspen's long winters. When the Gliddens removed a few of the siding boards to make repairs, the sawdust insulation inside tumbled out, just like a Victorian lady losing her ribboned petticoats.

The little front porch has white wooden columns topped with gingerbread brackets, and the porch light is a Mexican glass and iron star. The black, satiny double doors are decorated with lace curtains. There is a bell in one door, but it has not worked for years. Instead, callers use the set of decorative bells at the side which jangle loudly enough to bring someone to answer. The house number 232 on the glass above the doors is the original decorative type.

If the outside of the house is a faithfully preserved Victorian, the inside over the years has been made modern and comfortable, a characteristic not always found in Victorian homes. Through the front doors is a cheery entrance hall with an old-fashioned hat rack. While most Victorian stairs crouched along a side wall, the staircase in the Glidden house twists for a couple of steps then climbs brazenly up the back wall.

Gossamer embroidered curtains with glass flower tieback.

Carved fireplace panel.

The living room to the right of the foyer once was two small parlors, but the dividing wall was torn out, resulting in a sizeable room with twelve-foot ceilings. The archways to two bay windows are painted white and gold, and the windows hung with sheer embroidered curtains held with glass flower tiebacks.

The fireplace, once yellow tile, was painted black, and its carved wood decoration white. One entire wall is bookshelves containing a collection of Luke Short novels as well as mining era guns. Behind the room is a bedroom and bath.

In back of the foyer is the dining room, and beyond that is a pantry, a kitchen, and a back porch. Upstairs are three bedrooms, which are surprisingly large for a Victorian home, and a bath. Like most Victorian homes, this one has no basement, few closets, and no extra storage space, so owners built a shed in back and painted it to resemble the house.

Inside and out the home has been happily, cheerfully decorated, belying its infamous association with one of the West's most famous creators of gunslingers and footpads. The little house resembles a little old Victorian lady more than a desperate buccaneer, a little old lady who has acquired a snappy new wardrobe, a few touches of lace, and put up a successful fight to stay dated but debonair.

Billings-Thomas House

CENTRAL CITY

When sixteen-year-old Gertrude Jenks made up her mind to travel to California in a covered wagon with her favorite brother, her Ohio Quaker family told her: "Gertrude, if thee does this unmaidenly thing, the family will never think the same of thee again."

The family never did, but Gertrude did not care. She was young. The year was 1859, and gold was to be found for the looking. Moreover, Gertrude was adventurous. The pair never made it to California. They settled in Denver where the brother got a job, and Gertrude kept house for him, not an altogether easy task. One day, alone in the house, Gertrude was sitting in front of the window rocking when a band of Indians came by, spied her, and pointed to their mouths. The quick witted Gertrude shook her head no then began talking to an empty chair out of sight of the Indians, who fled, thinking someone was with her. Her descendents still have the rocking chair.

Eureka Street (foreground) in 1900s, showing Thomas house at the right. (Photo courtesy Denver Pubic Western History Department.)

In 1863 Gertrude married George Nathan Billings and settled near the confluence of the Platte and the Cherry Creek. Not long after they moved there, Denver's treacherous Cherry Creek flood of 1864 rushed down on them, forcing settlers to flee for their lives. Billings told his young wife to leave everything. "I'll carry you, but you won't be able to take a thing with you," he said. Gertrude pleaded, but he was adamant. Only years later did he discover she was so staggeringly heavy because she had stuffed all the silver into her pockets.

After a time the Billingses moved to Central City where Billings, a carpenter who had operated a planing mill in Denver, opened a similar operation. The Billingses had three children, two daughters and a son, and when one of the girls, Marcia, married in 1895, they gave the newlyweds a home in Central as a wedding present.

The house George and Gertrude Billings bought for Marcia and her husband, Benjamin Prosser Thomas, was high up on Eureka Street, just a few doors above the courthouse. It had been built in the mid-1870s by Charles Hendrie of Hendrie & Boltoff Manufacturing Company.

Later it was owned by one of the principals of the Sauer-McShane Mercantile company, a general store that carried "groceries, hay and grain, queensware, crockery, etc," according to a 1905 edition of *The Western Grocer, Butcher and Clerk*. Thomas, too, was involved in Sauer-McShane and was described as a "very strong member of the company." He was more adventurous than the average dry goods clerk, however, and did a little grubstaking with the store's supplies, though his gambles brought him only a small return.

The Greek revival Benjamin Prosser Thomas home is a big yellow two-story house with green shutters. The house is subdued and understated despite its pink porch. The front door was carved by a Swiss craftsman and set with an oval pane of beveled glass, and it had won a gold medal in a competition. The door was a gift to the newlyweds from Billings, in whose factory it was made.

The front of the house is two-story while the dining room, kitchen, and storage area are in a one-story L attached to the side of the house. In back, high up a steep incline, stood the privy. Said one who had used it: "You could see all over town from up there—and all the town could see you." A sort of drawbridge went from a second floor bedroom to the privy for anyone who did not want to negotiate the stairs and then the hillside at night.

The inside of the house has a look of mountain Victorian elegance: velvet furniture, scattered bric-a-brac, silk opera programs, brass beds, handmade quilts, and an engraved announcement of the marriage of Baby Doe and H. A. W. Tabor.

Most of the wallpaper is original and boldly patterned. The paper in the front hall, for instance, generously covered with pictures, documents, mirrors, and a deer head, is a gaudy pink, happily faded, with big blue and aqua Indian designs. Despite its overbearing paper, the hall gives a pinkish-warm friendly glow.

The parlor is furnished with original furniture and mementos—a velvet love seat and four matching chairs, a table painted to look like inlaid wood, a picture made of colored tinfoil, a motto, "There's No Place Like Home." The original carpet with its green background and bilious garlands of yellow and red flowers, still glares up at visitors. The sitting room is dominated by an ornate old coal stove and garish Mexican weavings that have been made into draperies. An old sofa in front of a pretty double window that looks out onto a patio cut into the hillside, is covered with a silk and velvet crazy quilt, its pieces caught together with neat feather stitches.

Off the sitting room is a little office with a lady's chair—a seat with a back and only one arm so the lady's hoop skirt could fall gracefully over the side of the chair. The drapes hanging in the doorway were made from strips of fabric laboriously cut by little girls in the family.

The dining room with its glaring wallpaper is filled with Victorian memorabilia—a wooden soda-pop cooler from the Sauer-McShane

Sitting room sofa in front of the windows is covered with a silk and velvet crazy quilt.

Dining room bric-a-brac: cut glass, Red Riding-hood, and Baby Doe.

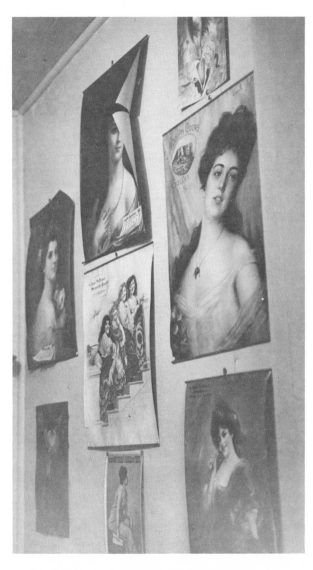

Girlie calendars from Sauer-McShane in "Saints' Rest."

store, an Edison Home Phonograph, a beer tray painted with the likeness of Baby Doe, a white fringed silk program embroidered with purple violets from the first opening night at the Central City Opera House. In addition, there is a large table, buffet, and coal stove.

The kitchen still has its highly ornamental cookstove, old breadbox, and antique kitchen equipment, including a turbine-powered egg-beater that screws onto a water faucet. (The house had cold running water.) The force of the water powers the beater. For years an orange and brown striped calico dress hung in the kitchen as a reminder of one of Gertrude Jenks' pranks. Her brother bet her she would not be married in a calico gown. Gertrude took the dare. She said her vows in the striped cotton dress, then immediately after the ceremony, stripped off the calico and stepped out in a formal white wedding gown.

Called "Saint's Rest" because of an old print of that name hanging there, the bathroom, added after the house was built, is decorated with old "girlie" calendars from Sauer-McShane. Over 100 were stored in the house. Once considered risqué, the calendars are more charming than tempting today. The house also contains many paintings by Marcia Thomas, which are out of proportion and horribly sentimental. They were painted in all seriousness though they are hung today with a sense of humor.

Upstairs are three bedrooms, one of which (appropriately the room with the drawbridge) has been turned into a bathroom. The medicine cabinet is a rectangular clock with the workings removed and replaced with a tiny shelf. Now the little door that once opened onto the clock's innards shows off tubes of toothpaste and razor blades. At one time the old house contained seventeen clocks. Some were fine old pieces. Others had been sent to Sauer-McShane to be used for promotions. A few, like the orange one in the kitchen in the shape of a piece of fruit, were intended to be hung in the store. Most still keep good time.

The master bedroom is elegant, containing an ornate brass bed covered with a blue and white star patterned quilt pieced by Marcia Thomas. She obviously did not intend that it be used on a bed because the quilt was found after her death, neatly folded and put away. On top of the quilt are pillow covers embroidered with "Good Night" and "Good Morning."

The Thomases lived in the house until 1912 when the decline in Central City forced the Sauer-McShane store to close. The couple moved to Denver though they kept the house and used it as a vacation home. In 1944 Mrs. Thomas' sister, who was living in the East, inherited the house. She thought of selling it but told her daughter: "This is the last thing we have in the West, and I don't want to let it go." She gave it to her daughter, Gertrude T. Tanner, who was so enthralled with Central City that she and her husband kept the house as a summer residence.

Since Mrs. Tanner believed thirteen was her lucky number, she named the house Eureka 13. Later Central City's lots were numbered, and the house's official address is 209–211 Eureka Street.

Mrs. Tanner—and now her daughters, who own the house today— kept the house as it was when Mrs. Thomas came to it as a bride in 1895. It stands like a home caught in time, gaudy and elegant, brash and pompous, decorated with affection if not taste, a relic of mountain Victoriana.

Brass bedstead in the master bedroom.

15

Gray Cottage

SALIDA

Salida's "Gray Cottage," named for the first owner, not its gray color, comes closest to being "steamboat Gothic" of any of the houses in Colorado's dry-land mining camps. Gray Cottage is a proper Victorian all right, with plenty of gables and dormers and Italian windows and is generously iced with gingerbread, but it incorporates several Southern features that make visitors think the builder or perhaps the designer had his heart in magnolia blossoms though his hand was among the Western pines.

The house was built by G. R. Gray, a mining entrepreneur who once was postmaster of Helena, a little town north of Salida. He worked the Madonna Mine for a time, then sold it for $42,000. Later owners took out millions, and as late as 1898, a Denver newspaper was reporting good shipments from the Madonna. His wife, Julia Gray, who was seventeen years older than her husband, was one of the first women in Salida, and had operated the New York Hotel. The marriage ended in divorce only a few years after the house was built. Gray left for San Francisco, and Julia Gray moved to New York. Before she left, Mrs. Gray deeded the house to its builder as payment of a $8200 debt.

The house was sold at auction in 1886 for $1,800 to L. W. Craig, a banker and merchant who had just arrived in Salida with his Confederate bride. Craig and his brother, Dodridge, owned the Salida opera house. The couple lived in the house for seventeen years before deeding it to Dodridge.

Unlike the trim of most Colorado homes, which appears to replicate stonework, Gray Cottage's gingerbread resembles the cast iron designs of the South traced in wood. Enormous inverted pineapples, a Southern symbol of hospitality, worked in wood, hang over the front stoop. The columns on the pillared porch resemble Greek revival architecture so popular in the ante-bellum South, and the shutters look as if they could close to keep out the sun.

The clincher is the front gable. From beneath, it appears like the front of a fancy Mississippi steamboat. Looking up, a viewer sees the

Pineapples are part of the design of the front porch.

The front of the house has a riverboat look.

balcony become a deck, the shuttered windows an entrance to the cabin, and the gingerbread, cast iron trim. The chimney sticking up behind becomes the smokestack. All that is missing is the captain, and it is doubtful that any of the prim Victorian ladies who lived in the old mansion ever resembled even slightly a profane, weathered, old riverboat captain. They did, however, have an air of Southern gentility and fine manners. One of them, Lucy Craig, was the daughter of a Confederate Army officer and a member of Galveston society. Said one longtime Salida resident: "When you went calling at that house, you always went with your gloves on."

When it was built, G. R. Gray's cottage was Salida's finest house, and the local newspaper, the *Salida Daily Mountain Mail,* kept a running account of the building progress:

"Timber is on the ground for Gray's new residence." (March 20, 1882.)

"Lumber is all on the ground for Gray's new residence . . ." (April 4, 1882.)

"Gray will be in his new residence in two weeks. When completed it will be a daisy." (June 26, 1882.)

After the house was finished and the Grays moved in, the paper carried an impressively long article about the home entitled "A Fine Cottage." The writer called the house the nicest in Chaffee County and claimed the carpentry was the finest outside Denver, ". . . first-class in every respect."

Despite its languid Southern look outside, Gray's Cottage is Yankee prim and proper within. No spacious entrance hall and flowing staircase but a slim utilitarian foyer with narrow stairs. The hall is finished in oak and bird's-eye maple and trimmed with black walnut. The sides of the stairs are decorated with a curling design in raised wood.

When built, the house had six rooms on the first floor, but one of them seems to have disappeared. Today there are five. The parlor is a large room to the west of the foyer and once was formally darkened with louvers, which later were moved to the cellar then to the library. The twelve foot ceiling has plaster medallions at the base of silver and crystal chandeliers. Besides two chandeliers in the parlor, there are chandeliers in the dining room, library, and foyer.

Behind the parlor, separated from it by twelve-foot glass paneled folding doors, is the dining room. Both parlor and dining room originally were painted brown, chocolate, black, carmine, and gold. Across the hall from the parlor is a library and behind it a kitchen and storeroom. Upstairs are four bedrooms and a bath with a graceful old marble sink.

The *Daily Mountain Mail*, in its 1882 article on Gray's cottage, stated: "Mr. and Mrs. Gray have the neatest home in the country, and we hope that they may live in it and be happy during the many long years that their present state of good health forbodes."

The Grays, of course, found neither happiness nor long life in their steamboat Gothic cottage, but succeeding owners, including the current residents, who have had the house placed on the National Register of Historic Sites, have found Gray's Cottage a happy home. Summed up a member of the Craig family who spent many years there: "It was a charming home, full of happy memories."

Crystal and silver chandelier in the parlor—one of five in the home.

16

William Forman home

BRECKENRIDGE

Life was hard in Breckenridge, just as it was in other mountain mining towns. When men struck it rich, they moved someplace where the living was lush—Georgetown, for instance, or glittering, sophisticated Denver. But until the strike, which they expected momentarily, the miners plodded along, sleeping in dirty shanties and tents.

Towns were built by more realistic people, those who had come to the mountains to take jobs in the courthouse or the country store. They did not expect to strike it rich. They wanted to earn a decent living, and they were the ones who established homes.

Such a man was William Forman, who was Summit County's clerk and recorder for many years. Forman was "common, ordinary, everyday," according to Bertha Biggins and Freda Dodge, sisters who lived in Breckenridge and as young girls worked for the Forman family. The house, however, is more than ordinary. Solid and substantial, like Forman, it is a handsome yellow American Gothic structure with white trim, a dainty iron fence, and a low gate with a plate bearing the name Forman. From its high vantage point on the highest street in town, the house looks out over Breckenridge to lofty Peak Eight of the Tenmile Range. The house bears touches of elegance with a huge square bay in front decorated with wooden panels beneath the windows and diamond shapes above. Latticework, scrollwork, and fancy cornices trim the front porch while the back porch, serviceably glassed in, is made of tongue-in-groove siding.

The house's sunny yellow appearance is deceiving, for inside, the Forman house is dark and formal. The first floor is a maze of rooms— a sitting room, dining room, bedroom, maid's room, kitchen, bath, and conservatory, which, despite its small size, once held a grand piano. Three bedrooms are on the second floor.

Though the house has been repapered many times, the maid's room, long used for storage, has its original wall covering of striped paper with gold bedecked tulips and a lavish border of blue-green flowers. Paper in the Forman house and most other Breckenridge residences was glued to cheesecloth tacked to board walls, and after a time the paper sagged ominously. Walls in the kitchen are covered with oilcloth, which also sags, above tongue-in-groove wainscoting.

Furniture was expensive and heavy, which made the small rooms appear even more cramped. While the Formans rarely entertained, except for sewing bees, the family had elegant silver and cut crystal. And the kitchen was equipped with the latest in Victorian gadgetry

Latticework trim on the front porch screens the view of Peak Eight.

—for instance, an elaborate compartmentalized steel cabinet fitted with kettles and heated stones: an early day steam table.

Mrs. Forman was a pleasant woman, recalled Bertha Biggins and Freda Dodge, who worked for her after school and on Saturdays for a few dollars a week. But she was "hostile if you broke a dish," said one. Mrs. Forman's work was lined up years in advance—Monday, wash; Tuesday, iron; Friday, polish silver. The Formans kept cows, and the hired girls were expected to scrub the kitchen floor once a week with milk.

Like most of their contemporaries, the Formans lived quiet, obscure lives. Few people remember them though the mark they left was more permanent than that of many of the miners. The prospectors and promoters came for what they could take from the land. The Formans and their kind made a more lasting contribution. They planted flowers on the bleak hills. They built houses on the harsh slopes. They turned the desolate, forbidding mountains into a homeland.

Wallpaper in the maid's room has a bright blue-green and brown border.

17

George E. King home

LEADVILLE

Leadville architect George E. King liked mansard roofs. He designed a smart one for the Leadville courthouse cupola, and he put an elegant one on the Tabor Grand Hotel (later the Vendome), the handsome brick hostelry on Harrison Avenue that played host to charlatans and silver kings during the days when Leadville was the wickedest city on earth.

King liked mansard roofs so much he designed two of them for his funny little topheavy house on Capitol Hill overlooking the Tabor Grand—one on the second floor, one on the cupola.

King finished his home in 1880 and occupied it through 1885. The following owner was A. Brisbois, who operated the Brisbois Photography Gallery on Harrison Avenue. Not long after the house was finished, the *Leadville Weekly Democrat,* on January 1, 1881, ran a front page full of pictures of Leadville's new buildings, including the King House. An article in the paper elaborated:

> Among the many new and beautiful residences erected during the year none are more tasteful and elegant than that of Mr. George E. King, the well known architect and builder. This handsome house is on Capitol hill, and gives evidence of the superior skill of its owner as an architect. Mr. King drew the plans for nearly all Leadville's best buildings, including the fine new court house and school house. As an architect he has no superior in our city and is well deserving of the prominence he has gained in his profession.

Tasteful, perhaps. Elegant, certainly. Victorian, undeniably. A third of the front facade is a tower, with the outsize cupola, which appears like a top-heavy top hat, held up by brackets. Round head Italian windows, similar to windows in the Tabor Grand, jut out of the second floor; bull's eye windows poke out of the cupola.

The house probably was built of frame, though an early account calls it brick. Later owners covered it with composition siding, but that has been removed in a recent restoration, and the house today is clapboard, painted tan with dark brown trim. King also added a jaunty iron fence that encircled the house.

Remodeling over a 100 year period destroyed much of the house's interior Victorian character though present owners are restoring

An 1880 photograph shows the King house under construction.
(Photograph courtesy Colorado Historical Society.)

Windows of the Tabor Grand Hotel are similar to those on the King house.

much of the former charm. The foyer is long and narrow with a slim staircase along one side. Its mahogany banister, anchored by a handsome decorative newel post, once was called the most expensive piece of wood in Leadville because of its intricate millwork. Paneling at the side of the stairs, which later was painted, is mahogany, too. The hall, like the rest of the house, had gaslights originally, and the tiny gas pipes still are in the walls.

The living room with its high ceiling is surprisingly bright for such a brooding Victorian house. King probably shut out the light with heavy velvet drapes held back with tassels and with dark, overpowering wallpaper. Current owners have placed filmy lace curtains at the windows.

King's architectural advertisement in the 1880 Leadville Directory.
(Photograph courtesy Colorado Historical Society.)

GEO. E. KING,

Architect

—AND—

SUPERINTENDENT,

OFFICE:

Front Room over Haswell's Drug Store,

116 HARRISON AVE.,

LOCK BOX 2214.

Leadville, Colorado.

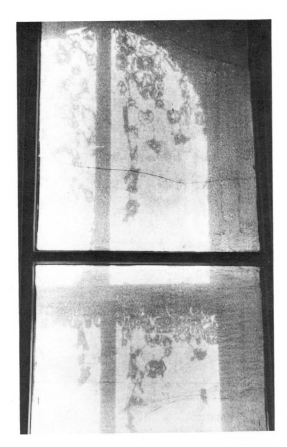

Dormer window at the top of the stairs appears to be etched with morning glories.

The dining room, the only other room on the first floor when the house was built, probably served as a kitchen. A lean-to or porch later was enclosed to make up today's kitchen. Strangely enough for such a tiny house, the King home had a back stairway, very narrow and steep, running from the dining room to the bedroom above. Because of the staircase and the diminutive size of the house, one owner speculated the home was built for a bachelor and his servant; but the property was listed in courthouse records under the names of both Harriet and George King.

For years the dormer window high over the landing on the front stairs appeared to be etched with drooping morning glory vines, which were visible only when the morning sun or bright moonlight hit the glass. One practical resident suspected that the inaccessible window was decorated so it would not show dirt. Apparently it was not cleaned very often; when the owners scrubbed the window recently they discovered the "flowers" really were grimy bits of decorative paper that had been glued to the window years ago and had partially crumbled off.

There are three bedrooms upstairs, but the smallest one has been turned into a bathroom, replacing the original bathroom, a fancy privy out back. The small back bedroom was for the servant, if there was a servant. The large bedroom was the Kings', and off it is the tiny room under the cupola, big enough for a single bed but generally used as a closet. A trap door in the ceiling opens into the cupola, which is used for storage.

Some Leadville residents say the cupola was built as a lookout for Indians, but later owners scoff at the idea, saying boys who once lived there made up the story for their friends. It is a believable tale, however. The quaint little George King house is one that invites stories.

George King house, 1982, after extensive restoration. *(Photograph courtesy Kendal Atchison.)*

18

Bloom House

TRINIDAD

When Frank G. Bloom left Pennsylvania to make his way in the West, he promised Sarah Thatcher he would come back with enough of a fortune to marry her. Bloom was persistent, Sarah was patient, and three years later Bloom returned for his bride.

To reach Colorado, Bloom had signed on as a cook for a wagon train, but when one of the drivers, who knew little about horses, tasted Bloom's biscuits, he declared he could do a better job, so the two traded assignments, much to the satisfaction of the other members of the train. Once in Colorado, Bloom opened a trading post near Canon City with Sarah's brothers, John and Mahlon Thatcher. The partners traded pelts brought in by the Indians for provisions and occasionally swapped cattle raised by local ranchers for supplies, and in time the partners built up a small herd.

In 1867 the Thatcher brothers moved to Pueblo to enter the banking business and to found one of the state's banking dynasties. Bloom moved his store to Trinidad and used the small herd of cattle as the nucleus of an immense cattle empire. Within a few years cattle bearing the Bloom Cattle Company's diamond A and circle diamond brands ranged from the Purgatoire River in southern Colorado to the Milk River in Montana. Later Bloom had interests in both coal mining and banking.

Bloom married Sarah Thatcher in 1869 and took her by train, then stage (where one of their traveling companions was General George A. Custer) to Colorado. Trinidad was primitive. The Blooms were one of only a handful of white couples in the town, and despite the fact that her husband owned a store, Sarah Bloom had to make do with very little. She once wished she could have a few apples, and Bloom surprised her with a small sack of them, enough to fill a small dishpan; she later found out they cost $7.50.

In 1882 the Blooms began their Victorian home, built from plans they had selected in an architectural journal, an elegant French style mansion that is unusual not only for Trinidad with its humble adobe architecture but for the rest of Colorado as well. The three-story house with cupola was built of locally made reddish-pink brick; the corners are accented with native stone quoins. Bright green shutters shade the windows, and grillework etches each story.

Originally the house had two small porches on either side of the tower, which were reached through the parlor and sitting room windows. Panels beneath each window opened up to turn the windows into doorways. Shortly after the house was built, the Blooms decided to enlarge the porches and turned them into a veranda circling three-fourths of the house.

Atop the cupola is a weathervane cow that once stood on the two-story brick barn at the rear of the house. Always up-to-date on agricultural methods, Bloom built a fancy brick chicken house as well. Alberta Bloom Iliff, the only one of the four Bloom children to live to adulthood, recalled many years later that as a little girl, even before she had learned to read and write, she had a tiny account book in which she kept track of the number of eggs laid each day.

The front doors of the mansion are handsomely carved with a diamond-in-diamond design and fitted with ornate brass knobs and cast-iron hinges. They lead into a hall with the parlor to the right and the sitting room to the left. The parlor originally was furnished with pieces the Blooms purchased on their honeymoon in Saint Louis, many of them upholstered in velvet and brocade. The grandfather clock that had been in the family nearly 200 years stands in the parlor today. Ceilings in the room are sixteen feet high, an appropriate height,

Marble-topped washstand in the Bloom bedroom displays antique toilet articles.

Bloom believed. When his daughter built a house in Denver in 1900, in fact, Bloom thought her ten-and-a-half-foot ceilings depressingly low.

Both the parlor and sitting room have doors and woodwork that is handgrained to simulate more expensive wood and fireplaces painted to imitate marble.

The sitting room where the family gathered to read or talk had a library table in the middle of the room with a gas lamp hanging over it that could be raised or lowered. Young Alberta Bloom remembered studying there, frequently turning to her mother for help in mathematics. Frank Bloom was president of the school board, and his daughter once refused to go to school because her classmates said the only reason she got good grades was that her father signed the teachers' checks.

The Bloom home had only one stairway, made of black walnut, and the Blooms were intrigued that a single staircase could accommodate both family and servants, though later they wished for a second staircase. Apparently the egalitarian stairway worked better in the architectural journal.

The second floor contains four bedrooms and a bath. One room has been restored as Bloom's study with his rolltop desk. The third floor servants' quarters has four more bedrooms. The house was so close to downtown Trinidad, where the maids could meet young men, that Bloom used to say he was running a "match" factory. Housemaids seldom stayed longer than two years.

A ladder led to the cupola, which was used merely as a storage area. But little Alberta Bloom, only seven when she moved into the great house, loved to play in the tiny room and thought she could see the top of the world from its windows.

The house was built on a hill, but when the city put in horse drawn trolley cars, the hill was cut back, so the Blooms added an eight-foot sandstone retaining wall in front and around the east side of the house.

There always were plenty of pets in addition to the fine horses Bloom kept. Alberta Bloom remembered a smooth-haired Saint Bernard, which later was found to be a Great Dane, a tame fawn found by one of the cowboys, and a rat terrier that liked to go to church with the family. He would sit on the wall across the street from the house on Sunday mornings waiting for the family to leave, then follow along too far behind to be reprimanded and slip into the church to sleep under a pew.

Though well-to-do and prominent, the Blooms believed in simple entertainment, usually for family members or church friends. Several times a year the Blooms hosted the presiding elder of the Methodist Church, who usually dropped in unannounced to spend a few days inspecting the church and accepting the Blooms' unhesitating hospitality. As staunch Methodists, the Blooms did not allow dancing in their home, and Mrs. Bloom was shocked to discover her daughter learned a few steps in college.

Longer than floor length curtains with cobweb edging cover a bedroom window.

Frank and Sarah Bloom spent nearly fifty years in the house. She died in 1928, and he died three years later. After their deaths the house had a succession of owners, one of whom used the house as a tea room. One owner painted the soft bricks a bright pink, but the house since has been painted dark red. In 1961 the Friends of Historical Trinidad Incorporated and the Trinidad Historical Society Incorporated raised funds to purchase the house and presented it to the Colorado Historical Society. The house, which is open to visitors in the summer, has been completely refurbished and furnished with period pieces—from carpet sweeper to cradle, china tiebacks to children's toys—including several original Bloom furnishings. The barn has been torn down and the grape arbor uprooted, and in their place is a formal Victorian garden filled with flowers grown in Trinidad in the 1880s.

The house was called the Bloom Mansion after its restoration, though today it is officially Bloom House; neither name appealed to Alberta Bloom Iliff. Shortly before she died in 1967 at the age of ninety-one, she remarked emphatically: "It should have been called the Bloom Home."

19

Pioneer Park

ASPEN

When the wife of Aspen mayor Henry Webber died after a short, sudden illness, townspeople began to talk. When the coroner announced the mysterious illness had been caused by strychnine, the mayor was put on trial.

Local residents charged murder. Denver and Leadville newspapers reported suicide. Mrs. Webber, a former Leadville milliner and an Aspen pioneer, killed herself because of her husband, "whom she thought paid too much attention to a niece," reported the Leadville *Evening Chronicle* in May, 1881. But the jury returned a verdict of accidental death, and Mayor Webber was free to marry the cause of the scandal, his wife's niece, Julia B. Nevitt. In October, the two took out a wedding license.

The home Mayor Webber and his second wife lived in has a mysterious aura, and it is said to be haunted by the first Mrs. Webber. Set back from the street, the house stands all alone in the middle of the block and has a high spiked iron fence surrounding it as well as a double row of cottonwood trees stalking it. Because of the trees bordering the walk, the path along the front of the house was called "lovers' lane."

The house was built in the 1880s and for some reason dubbed "Pioneer Park." The name is stenciled in old fashioned lettering on the transom above the front doors. Both sides of the double front doors bear elaborately flowered welcome signs, stenciled when Webber built the house. The first story was Aspen pink brick, later painted bright pink, while the second story is a black clapboard mansard roof. A symmetrical house, the Webber home has bay windows on both sides of the front door. Two bay windows on the east side were eliminated when later owners pushed out the wall to enlarge the house.

Pioneer Park had two small parlors, which have been combined, and a library, bedroom, dining room, and kitchen on the first floor. Three bedrooms and two baths are on the second floor. Ceilings on the first floor are twelve feet high; walnut doors measure eleven. The living room ceilings have their original plaster moldings and the gaslight fixtures removed at some point in the house's history have been replaced. The house had chimneys for fireplaces though the Webbers used coal stoves. Later owners added two fireplaces, one of them a beautifully carved marble fireplace from the General Grant Suite of the Palmer House in Chicago.

Outside there is a simple round summerhouse at one end of the garden. At the other end was a long stable, now a guest house named

Footscraper near the front gate.

Gaslight fixture in the foyer of Pioneer Park.

Schweitzer Cottage. Dr. Albert Schweitzer stayed there when he attended Aspen's Goethe bicentennial celebration in 1949. In addition, a swimming pool has been added in front of the guest house.

Aspen legend says life was not easy for Mayor Webber and his bride. Webber was a jealous, suspicious man who did not trust his second wife. He suspected her of having a lover, and after brooding about her unfaithfulness, he determined to trap her. One night he told his wife he was going to Leadville, saddled his horse, and rode off. But a little distance away, he turned back and hid in the cottonwoods. A short time later he surprised his wife with her lover, who jumped out of a second story window and ran off.

Julia Webber, so the story goes, stood at the top of the stairs pleading with her husband not to harm her, but the enraged Webber pulled a gun and shot. The first bullet went wild, hitting the banister. But the second hit his wife, who toppled down the stairs, landing at her husband's feet. The righteous Webber rode off into the night and never was seen again.

There is a hole in the banister filled with plastic wood, and a workman once claimed to have dug bits of lead out of it. Teenagers who lived in the house surmised that if Webber had been standing at the bottom of the stairs and his wife at the top, the bullet would have gone through a partitioning wall in order to hit the banister, but there is not a mark on the wall. Then they discovered the wall had been added long after the supposed shooting.

Whatever the truth about the shootings, Henry Webber did not ride off in the night. He stayed on in the house and lost it in the 1893 silver crash.

Later owners, including jet setters and another mayor, Harald Pabst, have been nearly as colorful as Webber. The most renowned of them were Mr. and Mrs. Walter P. Paepcke, who were responsible for turning Aspen into a cultural mecca following World War II. Paepcke, chairman of Container Corporation of America, founded the Aspen Institute for Humanistic Studies in 1949 and lured Schweitzer to Aspen.

The Paepckes and succeeding owners have turned Pioneer Park into one of Aspen's most formal and most dignified homes. Only occasionally, on moonless nights when storms blow through the cottonwoods, do passers-by recall Pioneer Park's tawdry beginnings and the ghost of the Leadville milliner, the first Mrs. Webber.

Schweitzer Cottage, former stable of Pioneer Park.

Hamill House

GEORGETOWN

William Arthur Hamill was a Warwick whose specialty was senators, not kings, reported an early Denver newspaper. Hamill could have been a member of the United States Senate himself, the paper continued, but he preferred his position of kingmaker to Colorado to that of office holder. As a powerful Republican leader, Hamill formed political and industrial alliances with other Colorado magnates, including Jerome B. Chaffee, who was elected to the U.S. Senate in 1876 and once teamed with Hamill to crush a powerful mining combine they opposed.

Hamill's fortune came from the silver mines near Georgetown—the U.S. Coin, the Gunboat, the Old Missouri, and others. And he wanted a home that would reflect his wealth and power. The result was Hamill House, a pretty carpenter Gothic cottage gone awry with a solarium, stone outbuildings, a six hole privy topped with a crown (the privy had a walnut seat for the family, a pine seat for servants), and an opulent interior rich in brilliant wall coverings and polished furniture.

General Hamill, as he was called (Governor Frederick Pitkin once appointed him brigadier-general of the state militia and sent him to quell rebellious Utes), purchased a house which had been built by his brother-in-law, Joseph W. Watson. With Hamill's help, Watson built the house in 1867 at a cost of $15,000. A paper included with the house's abstract tells that Hamill helped Watson saw most of the lumber used in the home. Watson, a speculator who made several fortunes but lost them all, mostly through dissolute living, borrowed heavily against the house and defaulted on the loan. The bank foreclosed, selling the home to James Clark for $3,882.50. Clark then sold it to Hamill for $4,308.84. Watson later built an elegant home on Denver's Capital Hill that was purchased by H. A. W. Tabor and his bride, Baby Doe.

The Hamill House was owned by the Hamill family until 1915, though Hamill lost his money long before that in the silver crash. Later it became the Alpine Lodge, catering to Georgetown miners who paid $2.50 per day for room and board. During World War II it was turned into a museum. In 1970 the owners sold the house to the Georgetown Society Incorporated, which is spending $500,000 to lavishly restore Hamill House to its former splendor.

The original house before Hamill began remodeling. *(Photograph Courtesy Colorado Historical Society.)*

Solarium with pewter figure of a boy.

Hamill House was a simple two-story home with a central gable in front when General Hamill acquired it. He added an addition in the back as well as a third story to be used as servants' quarters, and a schoolroom with small, high dormer windows. Hamill built a solarium onto the south side of the house using specially curved frosted glass panels held together by cast metal bands. Inside he placed rare plants on a cast-iron tiered fernery that has a fountain with a cherub drinking from a conch shell. Outside he added a second iron fountain with cast metal lilies and rams' heads.

In 1880 Hamill began construction of an office building made from granite quarried in Silver Plume. Elegant carved woodwork and a fine staircase connected the three floors. But Hamill lost his fortune before he finished the building, and the staircase remains uncompleted. There are grooves in the handrail for decoration that never was installed. In addition, Hamill added a stable adjacent to the office building with living quarters on the second floor for male servants. Pigeons roosted in the turret on top of the stable.

Hamill spared no expense in making his home the most opulent in the early mining camps. The chandeliers are gold washed and ornamented with cut glass globes. Door knobs are plated with gold and window catches with silver. The parquet floors are striped with alternating boards of walnut and maple. The walls are covered with camel hair paper, and wallpaper in the dining room, which has been meticulously repainted by artisans commissioned by the Georgetown Society, is a blue, gold, and brown flowered design.

The first floor contains a parlor, dining room, and library in addition to the conservatory and kitchen. All are handsomely decorated with polished shutters and heavy, richly trimmed draperies at the windows and thin, brightly flowered carpets on the floors. The dining room carpet, for instance, is bright blue with gold flowers, while the draperies are blue silk damask with pink fringe. The library's red velvet

Hamill's office, left, and stable. Turret on top of the stable was a roost for pigeons.

Decorative lintel in Hamill's office.

Crystal light fixture in the foyer.

Servants' entrance to the six-seat privy.

draperies etched with gold spill onto a black carpet decorated with gold medallions.

Many of the Hamill family's belongings have been returned to the house, including the general's tufted red leather library furniture that matches the curtains. The house was heated by a cast iron furnace banked by two feet of red brick, located in the basement, but Hamill added fireplaces to supplement the heat. The parlor fireplace is decorated with tiles painted with pre-Raphaelite style figures, while the dining room fireplace is marble. When the Georgetown Society had the dining room fireplace disassembled and cleaned, it persuaded the owner of the quarry that had furnished the marble for the original pieces to reopen an old pit so that replacement pieces could be made from the same marble as the originals.

On the second floor are bedrooms, a bathroom with sink and zinc tub, and a nursery. The children were not allowed on the first floor and were required to play in their rooms or in the third floor school room. A 1974 fire that gutted the back part of the house revealed a second stairway to the third floor and what may have been a nanny's room. It is being restored to give visitors to Hamill House a glimpse of a nineteenth century servant's quarters.

The Georgetown Society's preservation of Hamill House and its outbuildings and grounds was done with the latest restoration tools, such as microscopic examination of paint chips to determine original colors. But it was restored, as well, using common sense. Workers excavated the long unused privy to determine something about the Hamill family's lifestyle. Six hundred bottles were uncovered, most of them medicine containers, along with the pieces of broken crockery and china. When the Hamill servants broke dishes, it seems, instead of telling their mistress, they disposed of the pieces by throwing them into the privy.

Charles N. Miller home

CRIPPLE CREEK

Most of the men who made their fortunes in Cripple Creek mines shunned the raucous little gold camp and headed for Wood Avenue in Colorado Springs or Capitol Hill in Denver. Only a few stayed on and built homes on Cripple Creek's posh Carr Avenue. Among them was Charles N. Miller, one of the ninty-one lawyers listed at one time in the district's directory.

Miller, who arrived in Cripple Creek early in the camp's history, was an attorney, but he made his money in mining, probably in speculation. An early day Cripple Creek guidebook reports that in 1898 Miller acquired the El Reno, the Comstock, the World's Fair, and the Hilda M. Mines, sometimes called the "Sweet Group," for $65,000. In addition, he was president of the Miller-Young Brokerage Company in Cripple Creek. The business floundered at first, according to a flattering biography written by *Rocky Mountain News* founder William N. Byers. The firm was "piloted through rather troubled waters at the outset, and but for the skill and far-sightedness of the helmsman might easily have foundered." It did not, of course. In fact, only a few years later it was doing $3 million a year in business.

Miller and his wife, Josephine, built their Cripple Creek home on Carr Avenue in 1896, shortly after Cripple Creek's two disastrous fires. Byers called the house "one of the most beautiful in Cripple Creek," and indeed it was. When most of the town's houses were jammed side by side on narrow twenty-five foot lots, Miller's home stood grandly, perhaps wastefully, on fifty front feet. Once a large tan and brown structure, now white, it is an imposing home with three large gables, spindles, latticework trim, scroll-sawn siding, leaded glass, a large veranda, and a grand bay window. In addition, it was built with a spacious entrance hall, large rooms, good-size closets including a special closet for linens, central heating with an outlet in each room, and an indoor bathroom.

The handsome golden oak staircase in the entrance hall is beautifully paneled, and the paneled newel post twists upward. At the first landing is a stained glass window in bright orange and yellow jewel-like chunks of glass. Strangely enough for a house that makes good use of

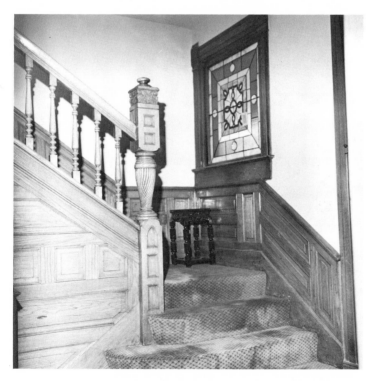

Entrance hall with golden oak woodwork, stained glass window.

space, there is no entrance to the sizeable area under the stairs, and owners joked of hidden treasure and old bones that might be hidden there. Farfetched as the idea sounds, it is not so improbable; owners next door who were replumbing their house found a skeleton buried under the foundation.

Just off the entrance hall is a coachmen's room in which carriage drivers waited during cold weather for their masters or mistresses who were visiting the Millers. They could shake the snow off their buffalo coats and warm up with gulps from flasks they carried in their pockets. There are benches along the three paneled walls, and at the end of the tiny room, opposite the archway, is a stained glass window in lavender, pink, gold, and green.

Coachmen's waiting room: entrance and stained glass window.

Old buffalo coat is a Cripple Creek relic.

The parlor is a large, lavish room with one wall a bay window looking out across Cripple Creek. Its walls are papered with handpainted murals done by a French artist. The fireplace looks like tile but is made up of small rectangular pieces of marble streaked with curls of gold. The parlor's gaslight fixture, long discarded in the attic, was saved from the dump by owners in the 1960s when a workman cleaning out the house asked if they wanted "that junk."

There is a sitting room, and through an archway decorated asymetrically with gingerbread, a dining room. The gingerbread, broken into fifteen pieces, was found in the attic and painstakingly pieced together. Along one wall is a handsome built-in buffet with drawers and glass doors with a molded border on top. On the opposite wall old lighting fixtures that once held both electric light bulbs and gas jets have been turned upside down to form sconces.

Whereas Miller may have been particularly accommodating to his guests' coachmen, he was a hard master when it came to his own servants. The call bell rang not in the kitchen but in the maid's room. And when the rest of the house was converted to electricity, the maid's room kept its old fashioned gaslights.

The master bedroom runs the width of the house in front on the second floor. A handsome archway like the one in the coachmen's room downstairs connects a small sitting room with its own tiny porch. The second floor contains three additional bedrooms as well as a bathroom with a porcelain tub and sink, its underside cast in a curling design.

The Millers lived in the house for only a few years, undoubtedly moving away when Cripple Creek began to decline in the early part of the twentieth century. In 1907 Edward Bell, who was sheriff during Cripple Creek's infamous labor strikes, occupied the Carr Avenue house, and he was followed by a succession of residents who have kept most of the opulent features of the house even during the bust years. But some accommodations had to be made to hard times. Said one owner cryptically: "You can ring and ring, but the butler doesn't come anymore."

22

Alonzo Hartman home

GUNNISON

On Christmas day, 1872, a tall young man riding a mule dismounted in a snowy cow camp—and into Gunnison country history. The man was Alonzo Hartman, a descendent of Daniel Boone, who had been sent from Denver to take care of government cattle for the Los Pinos Indian Agency.

Young Lon Hartman had lived for several years in Denver, camping at what is now 17th and Broadway, the heart of the financial district. But he knew the mountains and Indians and was well suited for the job of herding cattle in the drifting snow and freezing temperatures of the Gunnison area.

Moreover, he loved the country, and after the Ute Indians established a reservation to the west, Hartman stayed on in Gunnison, where he had acquired ranch land, and set up a general store in one of the old cow camp cabins. Hartman and his partner freighted in supplies over the mountains from Colorado Springs at great cost, but the store was a financial success because gold seekers who were crowding into the area were willing to pay exorbitant prices for supplies. To

100

supplement his merchandising income, Hartman acted as Gunnison's postmaster. He once told his daughter the reason he never smoked was that having to stand behind the small window of the post office and smell the foul breath of tobacco-chewing miners and trappers cured him of any taste for tobacco.

One of Hartman's close friends was Jake Hinkle, who had come to Colorado to seek his fortune. Hinkle told Hartman about his young niece in Kansas, Annie Haigler, a school teacher, and persuaded Hartman to write her. He did, and the two corresponded for some time before she came west to meet him. When she returned to Kansas, the two were engaged, and they were married at her home on January 29, 1882.

Shortly afterward, Hartman, who had spent his wages buying cattle, settled down as a cattleman on his Dos Rios Ranch, named because it was near the confluence of the Gunnison River and Tomichi Creek. He built one of the first frame houses in Gunnison for his bride, locating it on his ranch, a mile west of town.

Though a plain frame house was indeed elegant in a town of squat log cabins, the Dos Rios ranch house was made even fancier when the builder varied the direction of the clapboard. For the most part, it is horizontal, but under the front gable and the front window the boards were placed vertically while above the window they were nailed on in a herringbone pattern. The gable sported a handsome bit of ginger-

Original Hartman home, just behind the mansion.

The Hartman family at Dos Rios shortly after the house was built. Alonzo Hartman stands at rear; Annie Hartman is in white blouse. Their children are Bruce (front, left) and Hazel (front, right). (Photo courtesy Duane Vandenbusche.)

bread trim, and there was decoration on the porch supports that turned them into pseudo-arches. For years the house was painted a sort of Union Pacific yellow.

Hartman did even better with the barn and stable, which he built in 1889. The barn was constructed of brick, which withstood a fire many years later that would have demolished a less substantial structure.

The frame house and the brick barn were fine structures indeed but not good enough for Hartman as his cattle operation prospered. About 1894, Hartman, by then a wealthy rancher, decided he wanted a mansion, and he built one that for miles around was known as just that, "the mansion," and sometimes even "the castle."

The new home was located in front of the frame house, which was turned into servants' quarters, and was just a short distance from the old log post office. It was reached by an imposing circular driveway. Designed by the local minister, a man named Fuller, the house is a blend of Victorian motifs, western architecture, and church elegance. It also was a large, showy, ill-arranged house that cost Hartman the extraordinary sum of $45,000.

Constructed of brick, probably made in Gunnison, natural stone, and wood siding, the house is a rectangle with a huge tower, which is completely out of scale, on the front. The windows in the tower, set into round-headed Italian arches, are stair-stepped around the tower as they follow a large staircase. While the arched tops remain the same size, the length of the windows shortens until finally only an arch is left. There are seven windows and eight arches. The third floor of the tower has a conical roof like a dunce cap and a weather vane.

The entrance hall, by far the most imposing part of the house, has a commanding white oak staircase with decorative balustrades circling up the tower to the second floor. The stained glass windows along the staircase are divided into sections and contain jewel-colored flowers and birds as well as abstract shapes in apple green, turquoise, and orange. The windows are framed with white oak arches, and the keystone at the top of each arch is enhanced with a wedge-shaped piece of carved wood.

The fireplace across from the staircase, purchased at the Chicago World's Fair, is decorated with pinkish brown tiles that have a design of figures in relief. The hall held two large showcases which were filled with Indian artifacts, most of them the gifts of Hartman's Ute friends, Chief Ouray and Chipeta.

The entrance hall opens into a sitting room with a velvet-draped bay window alcove. The arch to the alcove is decorated with handsome wood filigree to match the oak doors. A leaded, colored glass window looks out onto what is now the kitchen but originally was a pantry. To the right, through an archway decorated with wood filigree, is the library. Both rooms have tile fireplaces as well as parquet floors. In

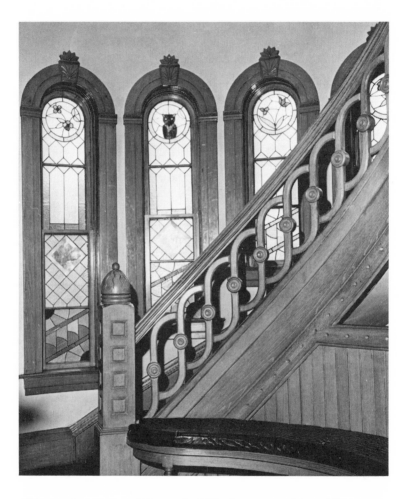

The staircase is white oak. Windows combine Victorian and abstract designs.

Waterfall painted by Mrs. Hartman on tower wall.

The tile in the foyer fireplace is Italian.

addition, there is a dining room with fireplace and a glassed-in play-room, which was added later.

The kitchen was originally in the basement, with food brought to the dining room in a dumb waiter, but a subsequent owner moved the kitchen to the first floor. The basement with its low ceiling is dark and gloomy though it does have a fireplace and a carved white oak staircase connecting with the one in the entrance hall.

There are three bedrooms and a bath on the second floor. The third floor turret is a white-washed room with many windows looking out on Gunnison County. Mrs. Hartman used it as an artist's studio. She climbed the steep, narrow fold-up staircase in her full skirts, lifted the trap door, and sat down to paint her proper Victorian pictures in solitude. No one remembers whether she had talent, but she was prolific, and the house was filled with her work. On the tower wall next to a window she painted a pretty miniature of a waterfall.

Hartman became one of the Western Slope's major ranchers, running cattle over 2,000 acres, but by the 1920s, after some fifty years in the cattle business, he retired. He sold Dos Rios and moved to California, where he died in 1940. Dos Rios was worked as a ranch by several owners until the 1960s when a development firm purchased the old place and sectioned off most of the land into vacation homesites. The ranch itself was whittled down to the size of a gentleman's farm with the still elegant mansion a sort of defrocked manor house.

23

Thomas B. Townsend home

MONTROSE

Thomas B. Townsend was a misplaced Englishman who did not much like the United States, especially the rugged Western Slope. Since he made his money there, he found it necessary to live in western Colorado, so he made the best of it. He built his home as far away as possible from his mining properties in Ouray and Silverton, choosing instead the prettier, more genteel town of Montrose as his home.

Surprisingly for such a staunch Englishman, Townsend chose American Victorian architecture rather than a proper English style for the brick house he built in Montrose. It was stylized eastern architecture to be sure, not the raw, gaudy, hit-or-miss carpenter Gothic of the mining camps, but it was decidedly American.

Townsend, who in addition to his mining investments was a founder of the Montrose County Bank, now the First National Bank of Montrose, built his house in 1888 on a former homestead, though over the years most of the land has been sold off. The house and matching outhouse are constructed of brownish-pink brick made in Townsend's own brickworks. He established the factory on his property near the Uncompahgre River, and bricks were made from the river clay. Most likely the plant was set up just to accommodate the house since it closed shortly after the home was completed.

The house has natural stone trim as well as wood in decorative designs. Built with two gables in front and others on the side, the Townsend house has three porches, one on the first floor near the front door, a second above it, and the third around the side on Townsend Avenue. At the peak of the copper and zinc roof is a metal hogback design.

Like the exterior, the interior of the house was vintage Americana with only a few English touches, one being the formal pine paneling along the staircase in the entrance hall. Once highly polished and shining, it gave the house a cool, dignified air. Unobtrusive knobs in the panels open them to reveal closets. The balustrades and railing are walnut and fashioned in a criss-cross design. The front entrance is wide and handsome with red, gold, and green stained glass panels in the doors and alongside them.

Townsend built his mountain Mayfair home on a center hall plan. To the right is the front parlor and through sliding doors is a back

Entrance hall with paneled staircase.

parlor. The rooms had wall-to-wall carpeting, though Townsend, ever the proper Englishman, disdained central heating, so the house was warmed by coal-burning fireplaces, five of them originally.

Only two are left. The fireplace in the back parlor is brown and white Italian tile. The pieces across the top of the fireplace are designed with apple blossoms in relief while the side tiles show tall asters growing out of fish bowls. The fireplace frame is oak with carved brackets and shelves. Sunbursts and panels are set with mirrors. The other remaining fireplace is in the dining room, across the hall from the front parlor. Made of cherrywood, it has wine-colored tiles decorated with geometric designs. In the upper outside corners of the tiled area are two tiles of a man and a woman in Elizabethan garb.

Through a pantry to the back was the original kitchen, now a dining room with two outside entrances. The doors have windows decorated with panes of glass stained every color of the rainbow.

Upstairs are four bedrooms for the family while down a few steps is a maid's room. The house was built with a partial bath. Rain was funneled off the roof into a cistern at the rear of the house, then pumped to the attic from where it flowed to the bathroom.

The house was wired for electricity though Montrose had no electrical generating plant. While he waited for electricity to come, Townsend lit his house with either gas or kerosene.

Townsend moved out before electricity arrived. Less than a year after he built the house, Townsend and his wife, Alice B. Cornish, whom he married in 1885, left for England so their child could be born on sanctified soil. Though Townsend did not return to Montrose to live, his descendents are still involved in the bank.

The house stood vacant more than ten years until in 1899, E. L. Osborn, a vice president of the bank, purchased it for $8,000. More content with Montrose than Townsend had been, Osborn and his descendents lived in the house until 1971.

Fireplace tile panels.

24

Pitkin Place "Gargoyle House"

PUEBLO

Winged serpents, impish gargoyles, wild lions rendered in stone, stained glass skylight, turret and tower, lavishly carved woodwork— all are combined in a happily opulent Victorian house in Pueblo.

Built about 1893 on land that once was owned by the Colorado Fuel and Iron Company, now the CF&I Steel Corporation, the house was designed by architect George W. Roe and built by contractor E. W. Shutt. Roe was one of Colorado's most prolific architects, designing dozens of buildings in the state. Primarily an institutional architect, he worked on prisons, libraries, and more than sixty public school buildings. But all that institutional work could not cover up Roe's innate sense of whimsy, which is evident in the houses he designed on Pueblo's exclusive Pitkin Place (now the 300 block of West Pitkin Avenue). The architect-contractor team of Roe and Shutt built six of the seven houses on the north side of the block (the seventh was a later addition). And the homes were so elegant they were featured on picture postcards.

The most decorative of the Pitkin Place group is the "gargoyle house" on the corner, made of native pink stone, probably quarried at nearby Stone City where much of Pueblo got its building material. The house features all the pretentious embellishments that Victorians loved to add to their homes and which Roe had had to suppress in his public buildings. There is a turret with a steeple top as well as a tower supported by carved pillars and topped with a battlement. Enormous archways are carved with flowers and leaves. A porch has checkerboard stonework. Impish faces peer from designs in the stone, and one saucy demon is sticking out his tongue.

Most impressive are the splendid stone lions guarding the steps. Children love them, and owners of the house say not a boy or girl passes without stopping for a ride. Local legend claims they roar only when a virgin walks by, but no one in the neighborhood has heard them make a sound. One lion, in fact, has gone to sleep.

The inside of the gargoyle house is as ornamental as the outside. The entrance is lavishly decorated with carved and paneled oak. The stairwell is a carved oak oval. Though there have been at least two weddings in the house, neither bride marched down the staircase to meet her groom.

The chandelier in the hall is a handsome silver piece with crystal drops and amber jewel-cut glass pieces. Above the door is a brightly colored stained glass window. Originally parquet, the floor was badly worn and the boards split, so the floor was covered with carpeting.

The front and back parlors have been combined into a single living room with the tower, which goes from the basement to the third floor, forming a protruding alcove. Glass in the tower windows is rounded, and replacement pieces had to be ordered from France. Each parlor was built with a fireplace, but one was removed when the rooms were combined.

In addition, there is a dining room and kitchen on the first floor. Later owners added a family room. The original portion of the second

Carved oak mantel is one of two that were in the living room.

floor has three bedrooms and a nursery. More bedrooms were added over the family room. The third floor is an odd room fitted between the tower and the turret, under the sloping roof. Its windows are strangely shaped, some starting at the floor and ending halfway up the wall. Though they blend perfectly with the imps and gremlins outside, the windows from within give the room a topsy-turvy appearance. In the center of the large third floor room is a skylight of tiny crescent windows. One has a white fleur-de-lis in the center with pink, red, and gold bits of colored glass around it. The third floor also contains a maid's room.

Pretentious but thoroughly original and with an impish sense of humor, the gargoyle house is a happy bit of Victoriana.

Stonework imps and gremlins.

25

Courtesy Western History Department, Denver Public Library.

Finn's Folly

CRIPPLE CREEK

"The Towers" in Cripple Creek was built because of an enthusiastic promise given by J. Maurice Finn to Theodore Roosevelt. Before a crowd of thousands gathered to see the man running for vice-president, who was making a campaign trip to the Cripple Creek mining district, Finn proclaimed: "Someday, Colonel, I hope you will revisit this great district and give Mrs. Finn and me the honor of entertaining the vice-president of the United States at our home, the Towers." Roosevelt promised Finn he could expect the visit the following year.

Taken aback, Finn realized Roosevelt meant it. The Towers had never been more than an enthusiastic dream. Finn, in fact, had not even selected the site.

Such an impediment was a trifling matter for Finn, a Michigan politico who had gone to Cripple Creek to seek his fortune. Finn was a slick lawyer, and before long he was engaged as legal counsel for Winfield Scott Stratton, wealthy owner of the Independence Mine near Victor and the district's first millionaire.

With Stratton as his patron, Finn, who had just acquired a third wife, was already spending a fortune for tapestries and Oriental rugs for the mansion he hoped to build some day. And Finn had built up a large collection of rare and costly law books as well as enough marble and bronze busts of American patriots to fill an art gallery. The high spending Finns stopped their extravagance only momentarily when Stratton fired Finn and rumors began circulating that Finn was broke. Johnson R. Barbee, father of *Cripple Creek Days* author Mabel Barbee Lee, for instance, told his family that Finn spent too much on tomfoolery. "The only sensible thing he's got to show for his money is a couple dozen cases of Kentucky bourbon," he said.

Finn was not broke, however, at least not yet. He switched his legal tactics, and instead of defending Stratton against lawsuits, he became the lawyer to hire if one wanted to sue Stratton.

In 1901 when Finn read a newspaper story telling that Roosevelt planned to visit Colorado later in the year and hoped to renew his friendship with "that distinguished Democrat, J. Maurice Finn," the lawyer was forced to begin construction of his house. Finn and his wife, Elsie Belle, decided on a site at the corner of Placer Street and the west slope of Church Hill despite the fact that the owner of the land, the city of Cripple Creek, was asking the impossible price of $3,000 for the property. Finn was resourceful, however. He proposed that the city council donate the land to him tax free since the mansion he planned to build would be a fine asset for Cripple Creek. The city fathers not only liked the idea, they gave Finn an additional $2,000 to pay for grading. The house apparently hit a patriotic nerve in Cripple Creek because the town's tight fisted banker, Albert Carlton, loaned Finn enough money to complete the residence.

Finn expected the house to cost $25,000, but unforeseen expenses such as $8,000 for Michigan lumber, the only material deemed strong enough for the frame, and the elegant oak paneling for the interior, nearly doubled the price. Whatever the cost, the Towers, three stories high with twenty-six rooms and an observation deck on top, was the pride of the district.

Identical entrances opened into a rotunda from each side of the house, and in the center of the two-story rotunda was a magnificent marble fountain adjacent to an enormous staircase. There were fourteen bedrooms on the second floor, each opening onto the balcony surrounding the rotunda, and the third floor was an enormous gambling room. The main rooms were named after Finn's favorite historical personages—the Abraham Lincoln library, for instance, and the Thomas Jefferson trophy rooms. And there probably was one named for Theodore Roosevelt, who was responsible for the house.

Because of the part Roosevelt played in the Towers—named for the towers at each corner of the house—Finn asked the hero of San Juan Hill to christen it at a magnificent reception he gave in Roosevelt's honor. Finn had invited nearly everyone in the district and decorated the house grandly even though the gray paint on the exterior was still wet, and carpenters' tools and scraps of building materials had been hidden hastily under the front steps.

With flags flying from each tower, the house was decorated with bunting and flowers and potted palms. A string orchestra played in the rotunda, and along one wall Finn rigged up a giant fresco of the Mount of the Holy Cross with a stream of water cascading out of the picture into an aquarium filled with mountain trout. Mabel Barbee Lee heard Roosevelt exclaim to Finn: "I say, Maurice, this is phenomenal. You deserve a Congressional medal for your ingenuity."

He never got one, of course. All Finn got for his trouble were bills. It was appropriate Roosevelt never got around to christening the Towers because the name never was used. Before the paint was dry, the mortgaged manor was known as "Finn's Folly."

Shortly after Roosevelt's visit, Finn, hounded by creditors, moved his law practice to Denver though Elsie Belle stayed on in the house meeting payments by renting rooms to school teachers. That did not last long, however. By the 1920s, Finn's Folly was too expensive to maintain, and it was sold for a few dollars and torn down for salvage. In the mid-1950s, the $3,000 lot Finn had beguiled the city of Cripple Creek into giving him was sold once more by the city—for $26 in back taxes.

The foundation of the Towers in 1964.

Courtesy Kendal Atchison.

"Swan's Nest"

TIGER ON THE SWAN

Along the valleys of the Swan River and up the gulches north of Breckenridge lie mile after mile of ugly piles of water-smooth stones, a mute memorial to Ben Stanley Revett, who brought dredging to the branches of the Swan and to the Blue River, churning up the streambeds and leaving behind monstrous debris.

Another remnant of the man, less permanent and less offensive, is the grand house he built overlooking the sweep of the Tenmile Range and the rock piles spewed up by his machines.

Revett, an Englishman, introduced gold dredging to Summit County in 1898. Enormous boats were used to dredge the streams, flat-bottomed dredges that perched on the water and sent clanging bucket lines down to bedrock to churn up the river. The gravel they brought up was washed to remove the gold, and the waste was thrown out on the river banks. The operation was an effective way of mining gold though financially not always a successful one. For Revett, dredging was a highly expensive investment that cost more gold than it dredged up, and Revett, never much of a businessman, generally was short of funds.

"He was always hard put to it to find money for running expenses," said a man who once operated a winch on a Revett dredge. "Probably Revett should not have built such an expensive house as Swan's Nest for his birds."

116

One of the birds was Revett's wife, Mary Griffith, whom he met when he brought her brothers to Breckenridge to operate the Wapiti Mine in which he had an interest. Revett married her the first day of 1898 and built Swan's Nest the same year.

The house was constructed near Revett's dredging operations overlooking the Swan where it turns northwest for a time before entering the Blue. The building is semi-circular with a large central portion flanked by two wings. The steeply pitched red roof is broken with sharp dormer windows, and a long veranda with a rustic peeled log railing runs the curve of the house. Beyond the house were a croquet court and pretty walks neatly lined with dredge rocks.

Both exterior and interior doors and archways were excessively wide to accommodate Revett's rotund figure. Revett was only about five feet seven inches tall but weighed some 300 pounds. He was such a large man that a Mexican laborer watching him work in a prospect hole one day dropped his pick at the sight and exclaimed: "Holy Mother of God! When this hombre meets his death, may it be near the graveyard!" Despite his girth, Revett was an immaculate dresser, and he generally wore a white Stetson. Women found him both interesting and attractive.

Swan's Nest's hall, as the English Revett called his living room, was, like its lord, of a good size. Across from the front door is a massive fireplace built of stones churned up and discarded by the dredges. Scattered among the stones are tiles with pictures of Indians hand-painted on them by Mary Revett. A chair nearby also was made of dredge stones. From the ceiling hung an elaborate crystal chandelier that at night looked "just like diamonds," a longtime Breckenridge resident recalled some fifty years later.

The dining room was in the central portion of the house, and Revett, a genial host, threw lavish dinners accompanied by several wines. After dinner the men retired to the library in the west wing for brandy and dollar Havana cigars or to the billiard room for a game. If the host was in good form, he sang for his guests. Once trained for the opera, Revett had a mellow tenor voice, and he was as generous with it as he was with his dollar cigars. When he was ready to perform, he would call the bar at the Denver Hotel in Breckenridge a few miles away—the Revett house and the hotel were among the few buildings in the area with telephones—and the proprietor would announce: "Gentlemen, Mr. Revett will now sing for you from Swan's Nest." Then he let the receiver dangle while his customers listened to the concert.

The other wing of the house contained a room similar to the library with walls and ceiling covered with tongue-in-groove siding. The room was probably Revett's office since just off it is a stone vault once entered through double steel doors. Revett kept nuggets and gold dust from the dredging operations in the safe.

Each wing had a stairway to a single room above, probably intended for the maid or the Japanese house boy since neither room connects with the rest of the second floor. A third stairway in back of the living room leads to the four bedrooms for the family and guests on the second floor.

Revett installed two bathrooms in the house. In one he placed an oversize tub and surrounded it with electric lights to effect a steam bath. One Breckenridge old timer claimed Revett drank as much as he ate and needed the steam bath to sweat it out.

Revett loved the Swan River, his dredges that flew silk flags embroidered with swans, and especially Swan's Nest, but Mary Revett found life there dull and uncultured. She spent the winters in San Francisco to get away from the long, harsh Summit County snows, but after a time she preferred to spend her summers there as well. Mary Revett

Fireplace is made of dredge stones and tiles hand painted by Mary Revett.

was concerned that her daughter Frances, born in 1900, would be exposed to the country's uncivilized element and grow up a ruffian. When the girl was about five, she and a geologist who was a guest of the Revetts, visited a nearby spring for a drink of water. After they got there, they found the cup kept for thirsty visitors had disappeared, and they had to scoop up the water with their hands.

"Did you get any?" asked the little girl.

"Not much, did you?" replied the guest.

"Not one damn drop!"

The geologist thought the incident funny enough to repeat it to the Revetts that night at dinner, but Mary Revett found it just one more example of uncouth life on the Swan, and eventually she packed up her daughter and left Swan's Nest and Revett for good.

His wife was not Revett's only disappointment. Always plagued with financial problems, he found it almost impossible to interest backers in sinking money into his dredging operations. Not long after Mary Revett left him, Revett, his fortune dwindling, was forced to desert the Nest as well.

He continued to live in high style at clubs and hotels in Denver and San Francisco, partly on the remnants of his fortune but mostly through the generosity of friends, until his death in 1929.

Swan's Nest was vacant for many years, preyed on by thieves and vandals. Once it was sold for $800 in taxes, and for a time it was the main lodge of a boys' camp. In recent years it has been restored, and unlike the rock piles that line the streams of Summit County, today it is a handsome reminder of Ben Stanley Revett.

27

Courtesy Colorado Historical Society.

"Waldheim," Silver Lake Mine

SILVERTON

When Lena Stoiber's first husband, a Denver & Rio Grande Railway conductor, failed to bring her glory and wealth, Lena divorced him and married wealthy Silverton mine owner Edward G. Stoiber. When he died, he left Lena a fortune which she spent lavishly on succeeding husbands, who continued to drop like flies. One of them, in fact, was listed on the passenger list of the Titanic, and Lena spent thousands of dollars on investigators who combed the world checking out the rumor that he missed the boat but seizing the opportunity, disappeared anyway.

He would have had good reason. Lena Stoiber was a volatile, sharp-tongued if attractive woman "who didn't forget her enemies," according to one longtime Silverton resident. "She never overlooked a chance to get even." She was known as "Captain Jack" for her prowess with horses and mules and her ability to outswear any of Silverton's mule-skinners, no mean feat since verbal communication with the stubborn animals was considered an art.

Edward Stoiber and his brother, Gustav, both mining school graduates from Germany, owned some of Silverton's most productive mines and operated them in partnership. The brothers were unusually close, and when Ed Stoiber married Lena, he moved her into a house just across the street from where Gus and his wife lived. Gustav Stoiber's home was among the most elegant in Silverton, a hulking, mysterious Victorian with a prominent bay window, a turret, porches, and fine scroll-sawn detailing above the windows.

The Edward Stoiber home is gone, but the legend remains that Lena ran afoul of her neighbors and built a house-high spite fence on the property line separating the two houses to shade the offensive neighbors' yard and prevent them from seeing through her windows. Lena Stoiber did not get along with Gus's wife, either, so the brothers divided their silver holdings, with Ed taking the Silver Lake Mine. (Lena Stoiber was hard on wives. She detested the wife of her brother, a Silverton mine manager, so much that she cut her brother out of her will. He broke the will, however.)

Gustav Stoiber house, across the street from the site of Edward Stoiber's early home.

Possibly to keep the two women apart, Edward Stoiber in about 1898 built an elegant house near his mine, an enormous brick structure that was formally named Waldheim Forest Home but called "the mansion" by everyone in Silverton.

Unlike the often fragile carpenter Gothic houses in Silverton, Waldheim was built to last. It was constructed with two-by-eights, two-by-tens, and even two-by-twelves. The foundation was of stone quarried nearby. The exterior was red brick, which may have been shipped from as far away as Philadelphia. Three stories high with a large veranda across the front, Waldheim, which served as an office as well as a home, had indoor bathrooms on each floor, a burglar alarm system attached to each door and window, and electricity generated in a plant located in an adjacent building. The ceilings were twelve feet high, and the doors, each with a transom, were nearly that tall. The woodwork was put together with square nails, and when the nails were pulled out many years later so the trim could be removed and reused, they left gaping holes.

On the main floor were a reception room, parlor, dining room, kitchen, servants' quarters, and Mrs. Stoiber's office. Stoiber, it seems, preferred to stay at the mine while his wife ran the business, the house, and probably him. Her air of authority was another reason she was dubbed Captain Jack. The office had a call bell system that rang in every room of the house. When the mansion was torn down, a man who purchased much of the building material claimed he got twenty miles of thin bell wire.

There was a large mirror over the living room fireplace and another in the office hung so Mrs. Stoiber could watch the maids working in other parts of the house. She brooked no shiftlessness.

Two staircases led up to the second floor where the bedrooms were located. There were as many as thirty of them, Silverton residents claim. The third floor was Lena Stoiber's pride with its game room and ballroom with a theater at one end equipped with curtain, lights, and even dressing rooms. The Stoibers frequently brought touring acting groups and vaudeville troupes to perform for them and their guests.

Waldheim naturally was the social center of Silverton, and the Stoibers gave fabulous parties and dances. Any dignitary visiting Silverton stayed at the mansion. If she could be a bitter enemy, Lena Stoiber could be a warm friend, and she was known for her graciousness and generosity as well as her spite. She frequently took food and clothing to destitute miners and their families, and at Christmas personally delivered toys to Silverton children.

After the turn of the century the Stoibers sold the Silver Lake Mine to the Guggenheim brothers (whose holdings later became part of ASARCO Incorporated) for more than two million dollars, and moved to Denver. There they planned an even more elegant house at 1022 Humboldt, to be called Stoiberhof. Stoiber was killed in Paris in an automobile accident, but Lena returned to Denver and completed the house. Once again she incurred the wrath of her neighbor and built an enormous stone wall on the north of her property which shaded the neighbor's yard. He measured the wall, found it was built in part on his property, and demanded she dismantle it. After squabbling over the wall for a time, Lena Stoiber said to hell with it and went off to Europe and more husbands. She outlived all but the last one.

Built to outlast any house in Silverton, Stoiberhof, home to a succession of Silver Lake Mine managers, was torn down shortly after World War II, purchased by its wreckers as scrap for a few thousand dollars. Parts of the house were removed by a former Silverton resident, Claude Deering, to be used in construction of a pretty little farmhouse bungalow near Durango. Lumber available right after the war sometimes was so green that it twisted, and Waldheim's scrap lumber was well aged and desirable.

Deering moved one staircase intact, and today, where it once led up to a maze of bedrooms, it now goes down to a simple basement. Doors were cut to fit the house, windows were trimmed to two-thirds their original height, and transoms were used as basement windows. Fancy gingerbread brackets under Waldheim's cornice were sized to fit on the bungalow and its garage. Deering purchased 13,000 bricks to construct the house and estimated he took only a tenth of what was there. Most of the furnishings in Waldheim had been stolen or wrecked though Deering acquired a silver inkwell engraved with the initials L. A. S., given to him by a friend of Mrs. Stoiber's.

Deering was not the only one to take away portions of the once magnificent Waldheim. Another chunk went to build a house in Montrose, and other materials went to erect a building in Ironton. Like its mistress, Lena Stoiber, Waldheim managed a number of marriages.

Brick House in Roaring Fork Valley

CARBONDALE

"The brick house" was a cumbersome, ill-arranged mansion that lived too long. It was obsolete before it was finished, in fact. But it was the most imposing house in the valley, built on such a grand scale that for seventy-five years passers-by stopped to gawk at it and wonder about the family that lived there.

The handsome structure, always referred to simply as "the brick house," was built in 1901 by Charles H. Harris, who began acquiring land in the valley west of Aspen in 1880. Harris had traveled over Independence Pass to Aspen earlier in the year and built a cabin that was used as a supply house. But he felt opportunities for farming were greater than for mining, and he eventually acquired some 800 acres, which he used to grow hay and potatoes and support cattle and horses. The farm was located on Ute land, and there were worn circles in the sod where the tribe had pitched tepees.

In 1886 Harris married Rosetta Noble, an Aspen school teacher, and took her to live in a one-room log cabin forty feet long. Later they moved to a small frame cottage, and at the turn of the century when his family had grown to include several children, Harris made plans for a bigger place, the biggest, in fact, in the valley.

Harris hired well-known Glenwood Springs architect Theodore Rosenberg to draw up plans. Rosenberg was a temperamental, outspoken man who wrote in a Denver architectural journal in 1890: "My activity of late was confined to plans that can not be built after because the owners wish to dictate style of finish, elevations and price. . . . I am not to be taught my profession by a lot of plainsmen and fools. . . ." Ten years must have tempered Rosenberg, because Vern Harris, son of the owner, recalled the architect kept drawing plans "until he came up with something Father liked."

What Harris liked was an enormous brick house with a row of tiny gable windows around the second and third stories. Not a man concerned with details, Harris eliminated a great deal of trim, inside and out, but he kept the grand touches such as the spacious, six-foot-wide staircase and the ten-foot-wide entrance hall. He liked space. The first floor contained a parlor with a tile fireplace, a kitchen with two pantries, dining room, sitting room, and two other rooms that were just rooms. There were eight bedrooms on the second floor, one of them an office for Harris. The third floor, which was to have had more bedrooms, was not finished.

What Harris did not care about were amenities. Though water was piped from a spring to a watering trough for animals, it was not extended to the house until 1914. A well just outside the back door and a privy, a two-seater, took care of the family.

The furnishings were typical of the day—big couches, a square dining room set, clumsy sideboard, each bedroom furnished with a bed, dresser, table, chair, and washstand. The only house that competed with the brick house for elegance was a few miles up the valley. When the millionaire who owned it went broke, Harris bought his cherry, walnut, and oak bedroom furniture, high bedsteads and marble topped dressers.

When the house was completed at a cost of $7,000, including furnishings, Harris invited nearly 300 friends to a housewarming party. A special train brought guests from Glenwood Springs, stopping on the track at the edge of the property to let them alight. Three orchestras and the Carbondale band, each playing in a separate room, entertained guests who danced waltzes, two steps, schottisches, and square dances. Said Vern Harris: "It was a terrible mob milling around, and they didn't all leave till the next morning."

Despite its grandeur, the brick house was not a happy place in which to live. The house was too big, and Mrs. Harris and her three daughters were overworked keeping it clean. The house was cumbersome. The rooms were arranged in a jigsaw order, and they were cold, especially the bedrooms, which did not have coal stoves. The fireplace heated just the parlor, and then only if the doors were kept closed, and the stoves in the rest of the house were inadequate. Moreover, the foundation was not strong enough to support the big house, and when the residence settled, it was lopsided.

Though she did not like the house—she had not been consulted about either the house or its furnishings—Mrs. Harris stayed on in the brick house after her husband's death in the early 1920s. A few years later she sold it to Mumbert Cerise, whose family did not like the house much better than had Rosetta Harris. In an attempt to regulate the heat, the Cerise family, who lived in the house nearly thirty years, took out the front staircase and boarded up the opening.

The brick house's downfall was its handsomest feature, its gabled windows. The roof began to rot away, and the price of replacing it, especially around the gables, was more than the house was worth. So the owners abandoned the brick house for a more comfortable home.

For years the brick house, crowded with old iron beds and empty cardboard boxes, inhabited only by a few bluebirds that fluttered back and forth in its vast roosting place, stood deserted like some outdated relic. Then in the late 1970s, with the roof and floors sagging and the walls badly cracked, the brick house was torn down for salvage. The most valuable material, carefully stacked for reuse, was the brick house's bricks.

29

Superintendent's house, Camp Bird

OURAY

When a group of English investors bought the Camp Bird Mine near Ouray they apparently felt they were sending their superintendent, William J. Cox, out to the colonies, for the house they built for Cox and his associates was enough to coax any luxury lover to the rugged San Juan Mountains.

The superintendent's house was begun by a Denver architect who proved so slow he was replaced by a Swiss man known only by his initials on the blueprints, E. H. B. Construction of the house was begun in the summer of 1902, the blueprints were completed and dated October, 1902, and Cox and three other executives moved into the finished structure in November. E. H. B. apparently knew what he wanted, and blueprints were an unnecessary formality.

A settlement of just a few houses today, Camp Bird once was a thriving community with a school, boarding houses, a reception hall, and several homes. Thomas Walsh, who consolidated over a hundred mining claims into the Camp Bird Mine, believed in giving his miners the best, and the boarding houses, which charged miners a dollar a day for bed and meals, had white maple floors, steam heat, hot and cold running water that flowed into marble basins, fire fighting equipment,

West side of house. Roof and turret are red.

pool and billiard tables, and a library stocked with the latest magazines and books. The men slept on good mattresses on enamel bedsteads and ate off china plates.

The recreation hall, too, was well equipped and had a square grand piano made of walnut. It was obtained through a poker game. One evening two well-known mining promoters, John Hays Hammond and Harry Payne Whitney, got into a stiff poker game in which a piano for the hall was at stake. Whitney lost, and bought the instrument. Shipping charges alone were $1,500. When the Camp Bird Mine cut production and the recreation hall was closed, the piano was left to the pack rats. Later it was chopped up for firewood.

The Camp Bird was the creation of Tom Walsh, who realized there were rich gold deposits above Ouray and began acquiring claims in the

Imogene Basin in 1896. He named the mine for the noisy birds that were numerous in the area. At first Walsh plowed all his earnings back into the mine, settling his family in a house in Ouray. His only extravagance was to add a tin covered walkway from his cabin near the Camp Bird to the privy. Once his mine began producing heavily, however, Walsh launched his wife and daughter, Evalyn, into Washington, D.C., society. Evalyn, who owned the Hope Diamond, married Edward B. McLean, whose family owned the *Washington Post,* and became a confidante of President and Mrs. Warren G. Harding. Walsh sold the Camp Bird in 1902 for more than $5 million, and the buyer, Camp Bird Limited Incorporated, built the big square superintendent's house with a roof that fits over it like a bucket.

The house was designed with thirty-two windows and a number of doors, and local legend says that in certain areas of England at that time, residents were taxed for the number of windows, doors, and chimneys. When it found the Colorado government did not care how many openings the building had, Camp Bird Limited lost control.

The outside of the house was sage green lap siding, which later was covered with a white composition material. The tower originally had tongue-in-groove siding, and so did the second story porch, but those, too, have been covered with siding. And the roof, which was made of four-foot shingles laid down in a pattern, was long ago replaced with bright red roofing.

The house was built with a good deal of tongue-in-groove wainscoting inside. The entrance hall has the siding on walls and ceiling, and the same tongue-in-groove even curves to fit the curve beneath the staircase. The grain of the wood was specially matched to take advantage of the curve, with the grain starting at a central point and fanning out. Later owners, however, painted the wood. In addition, the hall had a six-foot circular radiator since the house was built with hot water heat. Electricity was installed when the house was constructed, too. Residents of the house as well as the operators of the nearby mill were charged five dollars per horsepower per month for the luxury.

To the west of the hall is the living room, its fourteen-foot ceilings lowered to twelve. The wood fireplace, now painted, has a

Purpled bottles in the kitchen, found near the Camp Bird.

Living room fireplace with tongue-in-groove cover.

tongue-in-groove cover to fit across the arched opening since no damper ever was put in place. Beyond is the dining room. Across the hall is a library with wainscoting on the walls and a fireplace. The room originally had a brass chandelier with frosted globes. A doorway, added later, connects the library with the kitchen, which has been modernized though it still has a Dutch door to the porch outside. The top half of the door pushes up, like a window, while the bottom swings open. Winters at the Camp Bird were so severe and snows so deep that the laundress had to climb over the bottom part of the door and step onto the drifted snow outside to hang up clothes. Because of that, the clothesline is high off the ground.

The kitchen originally was equipped with a coal range, a rack suspended from the ceiling to hold pots and pans, and a soapstone sink so low that one woman who lived there said she nearly had to get down on her knees to use it. The kitchen was built without cupboards, and food and dishes were kept in a pantry, which now is a bathroom. Camp Bird Limited purchased twelve dozen glasses for manager Cox along with a set of ordinary china and another of rose-patterned Haviland. There were four china pitcher and basin sets for the bedrooms, too.

Off the kitchen is a servant's room built for Webster, Cox's manservant. There also is a small hallway with a fire hose used only once, as far as anybody knows. A new stovepipe had been attached to the cookstove, and it caught fire. The wife of the superintendent grabbed the hose and put out the flames. Satisfied that the fire was out, she nonetheless went down to the mill office and told what had happened, asking if someone would check in the attic to make sure no sparks had settled.

Mill superintendent's house, designed by the same architect.

"That was all those men needed to take half a day off," she said. The mill workers inspected the entire house, spraying water on the walls and furniture, and ruining her freshly baked cake.

On the second floor are four good-size bedrooms and a bathroom. The master bedroom has a tiny sitting room in the tower. The top of the tower, however, is empty. There is a cellar, but it is unfinished and fills with water during spring runoffs.

At the same time Camp Bird Limited built the elegant country home for its mine superintendent, its architect designed a home for the mill superintendent and three smaller houses for other employees. Looking like a poor cousin of the big house, the mill superintendent's home has the same steep-pitched red roof and small veranda in front.

Clustered together at the end of a five mile shelf road that winds its way high above the swirling Uncompahgre River, the little group of houses, dwarfed by the adjacent mine buildings, is all that remains of the busy town that once fed one of America's richest gold mines.

Camp Bird Mill.

John Cleveland Osgood's "Cleveholm"

REDSTONE

John Cleveland Osgood was a turn of the century financial titan who lived in baronial splendor. As a coal mining magnate, he controlled hundreds of men. He fought John "Bet-a-Million" Gates and J. P. Morgan, hunted with Theodore Roosevelt, formed alliances with John D. Rockefeller, and entertained King Leopold of Belgium.

And like the East Coast robber barons he admired and emulated, Osgood designed a palatial home called Cleveholm; but instead of building it in Newport or Saratoga Springs, he erected it in the majestic mountains of Colorado.

Unlike the financial buccaneers of his time, however, Osgood was an idealist. In the years before trade unionism, he believed in fair wages and good working conditions and established a workers' utopia for his employees at the company town of Redstone. He built cottages surrounded with flower and vegetable gardens for married workers and housed single men in a fine lodge with a clubhouse. Osgood built Big Horn Lodge for company officials and guests, a church, school, library, and bandstand. He encouraged exercise and good diet and even banned liquor at Redstone until miners convinced him he had carried things too far.

Osgood was born in 1851 and orphaned only a few years later. He went to work at fourteen, and at nineteen was offered a job as book-keeper of the Union Mining Company. Before he was thirty, Osgood had taken control of the White Breast Mining Company. In 1882 Osgood went to Colorado to look over coal deposits, and, according to his biographer, Sylvia Ruland, in *The Lion of Redstone,* he paid only $500 to two gold prospectors for an extraordinarily rich coal deposit on Coal Creek, a branch of the Crystal River. Osgood organized the mighty Colorado Fuel Company, later merged with the Colorado Coal and Iron Company into what today is CF&I Steel Corporation.

In 1891 Osgood married the first of his three wives, Nannie Irene de Belote, who fictionalized their lives, including their honeymoon, in a Gothic potboiler called *Shadow of Desire.* Irene Osgood, with her dramatic career and rowdy ways, was a contrast to her industrialist husband. She once was asked to leave the Hotel Colorado in Glenwood Springs for unbecoming behavior, and she eventually left Osgood for a novelist. Osgood divorced her on the grounds of desertion.

The second Mrs. Osgood was mysterious Alma Regina Osgood, whom he married in 1899. The second Mrs. Osgood's origins were cloaked in mystery, but it was rumored she once had been married to Russian royalty. And she was as controversial as her predecessor. Shortly before she and Osgood were married, Alma Regina Osgood discovered a friend had taken up with a fortune hunting riding instructor who had neglected to tell her about a wife and children at home. When Alma Regina exposed him, the riding instructor shot himself, blaming the future Mrs. Osgood in a suicide note.

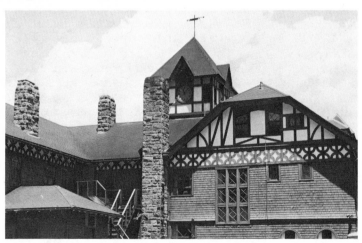

Redstone Lodge, which housed bachelor employees.

*Gazebo at the foot
of Cleveholm's
terrace.*

The scandal probably kept Mrs. Osgood out of Denver society, but that was just as well. She turned her energies to Redstone, encouraging Osgood in his paternalistic treatment of the miners and their families, and with a becoming sense of *noblesse oblige*, she became the town's patroness, bestowing favors and initiating good works for the benefit of her husband's employees. At Christmas, Lady Bountiful, as she was called, intercepted Redstone letters addressed to Santa Claus and personally selected and distributed gifts to the town's children.

Shortly after his marriage to Alma Regina, Osgood began construction of Cleveholm—the name was derived from his middle name. Built at a cost of more than $2.5 million, Cleveholm is a rambling castle a mile from Redstone with elegant formal gardens, a rolling expanse of green lawn with a gazebo at its edge. Cleveholm was the center of a hunting preserve stocked with elk, bear, and deer, to appeal to Osgood's game hunting friends, including Theodore Roosevelt. Fence posts with the dates 1901 and 1902 stamped on them mark the edges of the estate.

Basically an English country home, Cleveholm has touches of Italian, French, Spanish, American, and even German architecture. The towers and big clock in the courtyard, for instance, have an unmistakable castle-on-the-Rhine appearance. Inside, the home is awash with gold leaf and Tiffany light fixtures, polished wood and brass and leather. The exterior of the first two floors is stone, and the third and fourth are grey clapboard with Tudor trim under the eaves and around the tower on the terrace side.

The main entrance is off the courtyard at the rear of the house. A long entrance way has linen-covered walls, hand stenciled in yellow, orange, and green by a craftsman brought from Italy. There are light fixtures from Tiffany Glass and Decorating Company, a leather chair with a coat of arms tooled on it, and Battenberg lace shading the window in the door.

The two-story drawing room, which at times became a ballroom, has a massive handhewn sandstone fireplace with the Osgood coat of arms carved above the mantel. The coat of arms supposedly was granted to Osgood's family for military valor during the wars between Scotland and England. The enormous electric light fixtures in the living room are from Tiffany and match the gilded fireplace set. To the south of the living room is the dining room with ruby red velvet walls, cherry woodwork, and matching red marble fireplace. The library is a handsome, bright room, its walls covered with green Spanish leather. Emerald green velvet drapes match the walls. The bronze light fixtures, beautifully tarnished, are a contrasting green. The ceiling, done by

Walls in the entrance hall are hand stenciled. The light fixtures came from Tiffany.

Two-story drawing room with light fixtures from Tiffany. *(Photograph courtesy Western History Department, Denver Public Library.)*

The porch looks out over the Crystal River. *(Photograph courtesy Western History Department, Denver Public Library.)*

Tiffany, is gold and silver inlay, and the fireplace is Italian marble. Osgood collected rare books, and one of them, a Mark Twain first edition, is inscribed: "This is the authorized uniform edition of my books."

The music room has pale green brocade walls with matching drapes, and the molded plaster ceiling has an enormous crystal chandelier. The fireplace is white marble. Alma Regina was a musician and even composed a song she called *The Redstone Waltz*. A sunporch with a view of the Crystal River was furnished with comfortable wicker chairs.

Osgood had no children by Alma Regina or his other two wives, so there is no nursery, but there are a number of bedroom suites, some named for Osgood's guests. The large, comfortable Theodore Roosevelt Suite on the second floor was named for a favored visitor, while the John D. Rockefeller Suite, named for a less welcome guest, is smaller, stingier, and at the top of a steep staircase on the third floor.

Mrs. Osgood's suite has a marble fireplace, the only fireplace made from stone quarried at nearby Marble, Colorado. A tiny lace-covered window looks down onto the drawing room, and Mrs. Osgood, despite her egalitarian ways with the villagers, liked to view the guests at her parties to make sure a sufficient number had arrived before she made her grand entrance. Mrs. Osgood had her own linen closet since no one else was allowed to use her bed linens, an enormous wardrobe room with separate closets for shoes and for riding habits, and a private bathroom with a marble mosaic floor and sterling silver fixtures.

The most charming room in the mansion is Mrs. Osgood's personal maid's room adjoining her mistress's chamber. The pink and beige flowered linen-covered walls match tiny paired lamps, and the floor is parquet.

Osgood's suite is nearly as elegant as his wife's with a handsome mustard color tile fireplace, wardrobe, bathroom, and smoking room.

The basement is a maze of dungeon-like rooms. A game room is complete with billiard table, stuffed animal heads, and an Oriental carpet which covers the marble floor. Adjoining the house are servants' quarters, and the grounds contain a gatehouse, a carriage house, and an enormous iron entrance gate with rampant lions on the pillars.

Osgood's life with the benevolent Alma Regina was not an altogether happy one, and the two were divorced after about twenty years of marriage. Alma Regina, who died in 1955, never remarried. Osgood did. His third wife, whom he married in 1920, was twenty-five. Osgood was forty-five years older.

As his marriage to Alma Regina waned, Osgood lost interest in his utopian experiments with his workers. In 1914, in fact, Osgood became a spokesman for coal interests following the infamous Ludlow Massacre near Trinidad in which wives and children of striking union miners were killed by the militia.

About that time Osgood closed Cleveholm and did not reopen the country house until 1925 when he came back to die. After his death, Osgood's third wife sold Cleveholm and her husband's interests in Redstone, and subsequent owners, who scratched off much of the gold leaf and sold it, attempted to operate the buildings as a tourist attraction.

Today Cleveholm hangs on as a curious relic of an unusual man who combined twentieth-century social reforms with nineteenth century baronial opulence.

Walls in the library are Spanish leather inlaid with gold and silver.

31

Jacob Kochevar home

CRESTED BUTTE

A Johnny-come-lately to the field of jigsaw mining camp houses, the home of Jacob Kochevar was built late in the period of Victorian architecture—in 1913, in fact. And it was lived in for only twenty-five years before it was boarded up and left to the elements. For years it stood like a mute ghost, its blank windows like sightless eyes, blind to its decay, deaf to the tale told about it. The story may not be completely true. Nobody, even family members, quite remember what happened; but Crested Butte old timers say there is an element of truth in the tale told about Jacob and Maija Kochevar.

Their son, young Jacob Kochevar, who was called Jakie, built the decorative old home for his parents, who were living in a rambling house next door. Jakie was a fine carpenter, the best in Crested Butte. He had built the house across the street for his sister and ornamented the gable with the year he finished it, 1912, and he had helped to erect the three-story building he owned down the street. That building had been intended as a sporting house, but about the time it was completed, Crested Butte ran its prostitutes out of town, so Jakie moved in himself, and his family stayed on for more than fifty years.

The old Kochevar home next door.

Decoration on Jakie's sister's house across the street.

Then Jakie began construction of the new house for his parents. He erected a rectangular building and sectioned it into ten rooms, six downstairs and four upstairs. He placed all three entrances on the east side of the house, spacing them evenly along the wall and fitting in windows symmetrically. For the most part, the house is plain, but the side that faces the street was a sampler of Jakie's carpenter skills, and it has the fanciest, most ornamental facade in town.

The first floor, which juts out below the second, was faced with handsome wood siding and a double window decorated around its edges with knobs. The false-front second floor was lavished with scroll-sawn designs. Jakie traced designs along long pieces of siding, cut them out with tools he had made himself, and smothered the side of the second story with them. A few rows were decorated with scalloped edges. Others were edged with points. Then Jakie switched to sharp rick-rack dog teeth. When he reached the top of the building, Jakie inverted a big scallop, hooded it with a cornice, and placed the date, 1913, inside. Jakie Kochevar even built a wooden sidewalk, a coal shed in back, and an outhouse.

The Kochevars and their children had come to Crested Butte when young Jakie was about fifteen. Since Crested Butte was a prosperous coal mining area, Jacob Kochevar went into the mines. Jakie, too,

Scroll-sawn siding was done with handmade tools.

worked as a coal miner until he took up carpentry.

About the time Jakie Kochevar finished the fine house he built for his parents, Jacob and Maija were not on speaking terms. Jacob moved into the new house, but Maija stayed on in the old one next door, a long, narrow old house with a false front facing the street. Narrow verandas ran along the side of both the first and second floors, giving it the appearance of a commercial structure. With its doors opening onto the verandas, in fact, it looked suspiciously like a brothel, but the red light district was kept across the street.

Old timers are not quite sure just how long the separation lasted. One suggested it was only a short time, but another says the couple refused to have anything to do with each other until the day Jacob Kochevar died, more than twenty years later. But almost everyone who knew them agrees the two were often not on speaking terms, and before Jacob moved into the new house, they lived on separate floors in the old one.

Whatever the arrangement, one hopes they are spending eternity on better terms. The old couple, who died within a year of each other, are

The restored Kochevar house, 1982. *(Photograph courtesy Kendal Atchison).*

buried side by side beneath the biggest headstones in Crested Butte's cemetery.

Their two houses, however, have effected a permanent separation. Jakie Kochevar kept the house he had built for his parents, renting it occasionally or loaning it to family members. When he died in 1955, Jakie left the house to his son, the third Jacob Kochevar. Eventually it was boarded up and stood vacant for years until, sometime after Crested Butte became a ski resort, the crumbling old place was restored and once again is a residence.

The first Kochevar house, Maija's house, did not fare as well. For years it was deserted, its boards rotting away, its doors sagging, its walls and roof caved in. Then in 1971 the old house caught fire and burned down.

32

Congressman Edward Taylor's home

GLENWOOD SPRINGS

When each of Congressman Edward Taylor's three children was born, according to a Glenwood Springs story that may be apocryphal, a rancher friend presented him with a fine blue spruce, which was planted in the yard of the congressman's house on a Glenwood Springs corner. The trees reached maturity and towered over the splendid Taylor house, which was as solid and upstanding as the congressman himself.

Taylor built his home before he went to Washington. An educator and lawyer, Taylor had been superintendent of schools in Leadville in the early 1880s before he moved to Glenwood. Elected to Congress in 1909, he emerged as a powerful Western representative, author of the Taylor Act, which regulates livestock grazing on public lands, and served in the House until his death in 1941.

As befitted a promising politician who had made a modest fortune, Taylor and his wife Etta built a handsome and comfortable house on a corner in Glenwood Springs. Taylor purchased the land in 1900 and built the house in 1904. Later owners found a workman's scrawl on the bottom of a drawer in the dining room china cupboard: "Painted! Nov. 5, 1904." And during a remodeling many years after the house was built, a worker found a Star Plug Chewing Tobacco coupon inside a wall. It was good up to 1905 for one free plug of tobacco shaped to fit the hip.

The house stands on the site of an early brick school, which apparently was torn down to make way for the home. Taylor claimed that every brick from the school was used in the foundation of the large house. While the building cost was estimated at $8,000, Mrs. Taylor made so many changes in the plans during construction that the congressman confided to a friend he was afraid his wife would ruin him. Final cost of the house and lot was $17,000.

Slightly Southern in appearance, the house, designed by a firm of Denver architects, is large and symmetrical with a wide veranda supported by white columns. Originally the home had wood shingle siding, but that has been covered with composition. Though Taylor did not include a stable in his building plans, he did install big stone carriage steps in front and on the side of the house for his horse-drawn friends.

The front door is centered beneath a tiny gable on the porch roof. The windows above and to the sides of the door are leaded glass in simple, stylized designs like those a school child makes with a compass.

The home has many of the features included in John Cleveland Osgood's "Cleveholm" at Redstone, just a few miles away. All lumber in the building was imported—mahogany, for instance, was purchased from the Philippines—and local residents claim the building materials came to the United States on the same boat that brought the Cleveholm materials.

The big porch was a friendly place, and neighbors waited eagerly for the congressman to come home from Washington and sit on the porch swing, a signal for anyone around to join him on the porch to hear Taylor's tales about the government and the city of Washington. Mrs. Taylor was equally hospitable. Each day she gave the maid three dimes to be handed out to bums who came to the door. Word got around among Glenwood down-and-outers because there was a steady stream of panhandlers at the Taylor door.

The entrance hall is heavily decorated with mahogany trim cut in pillars, brackets, spindles, and egg-and-dart designs. All of it had to be dusted once a day. A picture in the hall of a little girl with a cat hung there for years until it was stolen. It has been replaced with one of Congressman Taylor.

To the left of the foyer, through a sliding door, is the dining room with mahogany trim around the fireplace. The dining room table, an oversized circular piece, matched the mahogany trim. Above it was an expensive crystal chandelier.

An arched china cupboard was filled with large, lovely pieces of silver, which Mrs. Taylor, a former boarding house helper, liked to display. Kathryn Senor, who was employed as a young girl by the Taylors, recalled the silver had to be taken out and laboriously polished in May then packed and stored in September. Since the Taylors dined late, the help seldom finished cleaning up before ten. She worked sixteen hours a day for a dollar a day plus room and board, and since it was the depression, she considered herself lucky.

There were two parlors, one for the family, the other, which was separated from the first by sliding doors, was reserved for formal occasions. The kitchen was a large room with plenty of space to prepare for elaborate entertaining. There was a large pantry and a back porch that

Elaborate woodwork in the Taylor foyer had to be dusted every day.

held the ice box, while between the kitchen and dining room was a butler's pantry lined with shelves for fine china.

A spacious staircase off the foyer was for the family while a plainer one just behind it was used by the help. A servants' call board at the foot of the back stairs was connected to buzzers all over the house. There was one hanging over the congressman's desk, for instance, and another on the dining room floor. The buzzer was a simple device and not uncommon in large Victorian homes, but some suspicious Glenwood Springs residents who were not used to electricity found the board an ominous thing. One insisted the congressman was "a smart old guy" who had all the rooms wired so he could listen and "find out where everybody was and what they were saying."

The second floor contained four bedrooms, a sitting room, and the congressman's office, which was furnished with a huge desk and two round, revolving bookcases. The second floor also had a complete bath, and the Taylors boasted theirs was the first house in Glenwood with more than one bathroom. The third floor contained more bedrooms while the basement was a recreation room.

The congressman lived in his home until his death in 1941, and shortly afterward the home was offered to Glenwood Springs for use as a library or museum. The asking price was a token one dollar, but the city turned down the offer. Later, when help refused to accept pay of a dollar for a sixteen-hour day, the home became too expensive to maintain as a private residence and was converted into an eleven-unit apartment building.

Despite the extensive remodeling and use by apartment dwellers, the house is still solid, which would not surprise Congressman Taylor, who once wrote a friend: the house "if properly painted and cared for, ought to last at least a hundred years longer."

The spruce trees have not fared so well. One was blown over in a wind storm in the 1970s, flattening the porch of the house next door and disturbing the roots of the other two. All three are gone.

33

Frank Warshauer home

ANTONITO

Amidst the earth-colored homes that cluster like mud hens in the sun swept towns of southern Colorado is a ponderous brown brick mansion, an elegant country villa, its gables tipped with bright Oriental designs. By far the grandest home in Antonito, this mansion nonetheless has a sad, melancholy history.

The house was designed and built in 1912 by Fred Warshauer, a German immigrant who had made a fortune buying and selling sheep. Only a few months before, an earlier Warshauer house had burned down, and the mansion was erected on the same site, a full block of elaborately landscaped lawn, tall trees, and a tennis court. "A peculiarity about the building is that it will have neither back nor sides, nor will there be any outhouses," a contemporary reporter noted.

The house is an H-shape, with the entrance in the center of a wide, open porch, which is flanked by two wings. The gables on top of each wing have an Oriental tilt at the edges and are decorated with bright Chinese red designs, red tile roofs, and little balconies.

148

Double front doors open from the porch into a wide reception room with a big English fireplace and dark oak paneling on the walls and staircase. Just below the ceiling is a red and yellow mosaic border of shields and coats of arms. Warshauer furnished the room with heavy oak tables and chairs, Oriental rugs, and potted plants.

Behind the staircase is a mural painted by Jens Ericksen, a fresco artist and muralist known for his work on the Broadway Theater and for Daniels, Fisher and Company, both in Denver. Erickson had painted enormous canvases for Warshauer's first house and was commissioned to decorate the second one for a fee of $2,500. In addition to the Erickson paintings, the stairway was lined with bronze statues purchased by Warshauer on frequent trips to Europe. He never traveled without bringing back something for his house.

The library, located in the south wing, was designed in a grand manner. Though self-educated, Warshauer was a well read man and a scholar, and he asked Ericksen to paint scenes on the library walls from the books he loved as well as portraits of the great scholars and philosophers he admired. Erickson obligingly illustrated pastoral, mythological, and historical works. He painted portraits of statesmen Benjamin Franklin, Thomas Jefferson, Abraham Lincoln, and Benjamin Disraeli; writers Charles Dickens, Ralph Waldo Emerson, Dante, and Voltaire; scientists Thomas Edison, Charles Darwin, and Copernicus. Ericksen

Gables tilt at the edges and feature Oriental designs in Chinese red.

tied the scenes and portraits together with elaborate, stylized green
and orange borders of laurel leaves.

Below the pictures, which are painted directly on the plaster walls,
is dark oak paneling; the paintings themselves are "framed" with
wooden borders hand carved in an egg-and-dart design. At one side of
the room is a fireplace alcove made of heavy oak and sandstone color
bricks. Matching wooden seats were built next to the fireplace, and
above one is a tiny window, its pane a rectangle of bottle glass. Warshauer furnished the library with handcarved mahogany pieces, part
of a prize-winning display from the 1904 St. Louis Exposition.

The north wing is a combination dining and music room with a
fireplace alcove similar to the one in the library. The dining room is
painted with flowers, grapes, and twining vines. There is a border of
beer steins around the fireplace alcove, and on the ceiling are musical
notes and cupids.

The second floor sitting room, the same size as the reception area
below it, is decorated with a painted border near the ceiling. There are
eight immense bedrooms on the second floor and half as many baths
with white tile floors and walls striped with tiles of Delft blue.

Warshauer had little time to enjoy his $70,000 home. In 1913 a
family friend found him in a shed on one of his ranches, dead from a

Reception room, shortly after the house was built. *(Photograph
courtesy Western History Department, Denver Public Library.)*

Stylized borders in green and orange and hand carved wood designs frame the paintings on library walls.

Paintings, done directly on plaster, were executed by fresco artist Jens Ericksen.

gunshot wound in his head, a gun in his hand. The local papers speculated he had killed himself because of poor health and mental strain. A special train hauled mourners all the way from Denver, and friends came in automobiles from all over the county to attend Warshauer's funeral. Two express carloads of flowers were sent by friends and business associates.

In 1918 Warshauer's son took control of Warshauer's $500,000 estate and managed the sheep business until he was killed in an automobile accident.

By then the elegant house Warshauer had built was a solemn house. When Fred Warshauer died, his daughter said, the house died, too. Mrs. Warshauer lived on in the place until her own death in 1944. But the magnificent house with its spacious rooms and elegant paintings never seemed to be a home.

More as an institution, the house was operated for a time as living quarters for nuns and used for religious activities and church retreats. For a long time it was poorly maintained, and a spirit of melancholia hung over it; dead leaves blew around the ill-kept grounds. For a time the house was operated as a restaurant aptly called "The Mansion," then in the 1970s it was turned back into a residence, and now, once more a home, it seems to be fulfilling the destiny denied it under Fred Warshauer.

34

John McInnes home

BOULDER

Lumberman John McInnes had slept in enough forest beds. When he retired and married a young woman many years his junior, he did not care if he ever camped out again. To drive home the point, he built the finest house in Boulder, and the heartiest activity he performed from then on was working as vice-president of the First National Bank of Boulder or riding the inter-urban to Denver to watch the stock market returns.

A Canadian by birth and a United States citizen by naturalization, McInnes had come to this country during the Civil War. After trying his hand at several jobs, he became an estimator for a Michigan lumber company, surveying forests and calculating the amount of lumber they would produce. Often he was out in the timber for weeks at a time without seeing another person.

When McInnes married the daughter of a friend, a girl he had watched grow up, he was ready to settle down in a house in a city. McInnes and his bride chose Boulder for their home and moved there in 1898, the year after their marriage.

In 1905 the McInneses completed their fine house on Mapleton Avenue, which had become the most prestigious residential street in Boulder. They selected plans for the enormous brick Greek Revival house from an architectural book. A daughter-in-law recalled seeing the same home in a Texas town. Erected at a cost of $22,500, the house was built by a Boulder contractor named Jenkins who chose speckled brown brick from Denver, marbleized white stone trim from Pueblo, and green porcelain roof tiles.

The house with its Corinthian pillars has enormous verandas on both the first and second stories extending around the sides of the structure, enlarging its appearance. The three McInnes children, Donald, Gertrude, and Gordon, all of whom attended the University of Colorado, waxed the porch floors for fraternity and sorority dances. On less hectic evenings, John and Georgina McInnes liked to sit on the veranda and talk.

On either side of the front steps are lions' heads that are functional as well as decorative. Their mouths are drains used when the porch is washed. McInnes liked lions' heads and used them inside as well as outside the house.

Staircase at end of entrance hall is made of oak chosen by McInnes. His daughter, Gertrude, was married in the hall.

The McInnes home is built on a central hall plan with the front door opening onto a spacious foyer papered originally in grass cloth. Large, massively framed oil paintings, many specially lit, hung from the walls. At the end of the entrance hall is an elegantly curved oak stairway, which Gertrude McInnes swept down in a long white gown for her wedding ceremony, which was performed near the front door.

Wood for the staircase was handpicked by McInnes, who selected the wood for the entire house. The living room is curly birch; the library, sycamore; the dining room, fumed oak; the parlor, Philippine birch; and the bedrooms, maple. Wooden rings that held the heavy green, blue, or maroon draperies in the doorways matched the wood in the corresponding rooms.

Georgina McInnes' reception room near the front door was a pleasant, formal room in which she chatted with guests who came to her "at homes." The little room was papered in panels of white satin wallpaper embossed with figures and had parquet floors. It was furnished with dainty mahogany pieces—inlaid chairs and settees upholstered in patterned French velvet.

Her son Donald remembered that a silver plate was kept in the hall next to the door for the visitors' calling cards. On days when she was not receiving, Georgina McInnes hired a hack and visited her friends. The McInneses owned no horses though they did build high carriage steps at the side of the house for the carriages of their friends.

Across from the hall is the sitting room with an elaborate fireplace with carved lions' heads in the corners. Mrs. McInnes thought the room too dark and in cold weather always had a fire burning to brighten it. Next to the sitting room is the library, an oval room with mahogany bookcases and a piano at one end. The window alcove had rounded glass and a window seat covered with green velvet cushions.

The dining room at the rear of the house has a built-in buffet of fumed oak to match the walls, and each drawer locks with a different key. The matching oak table with carved lions' heads at its corners, seated twenty. And over it, suspended by chains, McInnes hung a red and green Tiffany-type lamp. The house was wired for electricity when it was built, and to be sure the wiring was absolutely fireproof, McInnes hired an electrician from Denver at a cost of $50 per day to inspect it. In the early part of the twentieth century, electricity in Boulder was so temperamental, however, that the electric light fixtures were equipped with gas jets.

The rooms were finely furnished with paintings from Denver galleries and Oriental rugs purchased from an Armenian dealer in Denver. There were enough fine Orientals in the big house to furnish the homes of the three McInnes children.

The kitchen, butler's pantry, and an office alcove which held McInnes' big roll-top desk are included on the first floor. The second floor contains a number of bedrooms, which were simply decorated

Red and green Tiffany lamp in the dining room was lighted by both electricity and gas.

McInnes used lions' heads, like this one on the corner of the sitting room fireplace, on furniture and drain spouts.

compared with the rooms below. One bedroom, however, had a bedroom suite with carved lions' heads. The third floor is a ballroom. But since Mr. and Mrs. McInnes preferred simple entertainment, they turned the room over to the children for use as a playroom. The three McInnes children used the room for shuffleboard and roller skating, and later they held school dances there.

For all its elegance and the hired help needed to keep it up, the McInnes home on Mapleton Avenue was an informal place. Mrs. McInnes, who had been a kindergarten teacher, loved children, and they were always welcome in the big house. While she held formal receptions, she also gave club luncheons and church suppers for Presbyterian friends.

McInnes lived in the Mapleton Avenue house until his death in 1924, and while Mrs. McInnes stayed on, she used the house mostly in the summer, closing it in the winters while she travelled. Though they enjoyed the big house, neither John nor Georgina McInnes seemed overly impressed with its pretentiousness. Georgina McInnes, in fact, once confided to a friend that while she loved the home, she sometimes wished they had settled for a little bungalow.

35

Charlford

SEDALIA

A Scottish castle built in the year 1450 would have been altered by the fads and improvements of 500 years. Subsequent lords would have added plaster and half-timber work between the castle's watch towers and replaced slits in the walls used by bowmen, with oriels. During the reign of Elizabeth I, vaulted plaster ceilings embellished with Tudor roses might have been added, and as Dutch, French, and Portugese influences washed over Great Britain, foreign touches would have made their way through the castle walls. Over the years crude sconces would be replaced with chandeliers, and in the Victorian era plumbing and perhaps even central heating added.

The concept of a fifteenth century Scottish hunting lodge with just these changes and embellishments of 500 years inspired the design of a castle built on top of a Colorado mountain near Sedalia. The only difference was that the architect completed the work of 500 years in two.

The castle was built by Charles Alfred Johnson, a Denver real estate developer, financier, and socialite, and named Charlford for his two sons. Johnson planned his castle for a higher mountain, but when its owners refused to sell it, Johnson settled for a lower one nearby, which once had been part of a homestead granted to a Union soldier. To protect his view, Johnson acquired 2,400 acres surrounding his mountain.

Johnson commissioned Burnham Hoyt, a fashionable architect who designed many of Denver's best homes, to draw plans for the hunting lodge, which originally was to have been a vacation home. Hoyt designed a small Scottish castle with numerous outbuildings and a cobblestone courtyard. The building, begun in 1924, was embellished with a bastion, a crenelated battlement, and a rampart.

Stone for Charlford was quarried on the site. The pink, gray, and yellow volcanic rock was hand-hewn and then hand-chiseled by Welsh craftsmen who lived on the grounds during the two year construction period. The building included sedimentary stone, also quarried on the property, as an accent. Roofs are Vermont slate.

A long gallery leads to the castle drawing room. In the fifteenth century it would have been the great hall with a massive cross-shape table running its length. The lord and his guests would have sat at the head with their backs to the fire for warmth. And there might have been an ox roasting on the spit and huge mastiffs gnawing bones. But today, though it retains its baronial splendor, the drawing room is considerably less primitive and is furnished with contemporary pieces and fine antiques.

The room has a high, vaulted oak ceiling with carved wooden crosspieces. Walls, which are thick, handcarved rock, are a series of Romanesque arches with stone cornices holding roof supports. At one end is

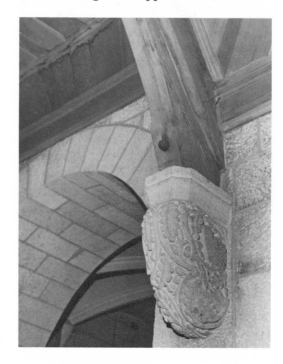

Only one of eight cornices in the drawing room is carved.

Drawing room has a vaulted ceiling, a
seventeenth-century brass chandelier, and a
carved minstrels' gallery.

a massive stone fireplace handcarved with an English design of squir-
rels, oak leaves, and acorns. A special craftsman was hired just to carve
the fireplace and the eight cornices around the room. After finishing
only the mantel and one cornice, however, he apparently went on a
bender and returned three weeks later to complete the job. The architect and the craftsman had such a row that the artisan quit, and seven
cornices remain uncarved.

   In a departure from his Scottish emphasis, Hoyt designed the fireplace screen as an art deco depiction of the American West with evergreen forests, Indians with captured Spanish horses, and prairie
schooners. At the other end of the great room is a smaller, simpler
fireplace, and above it is a gracefully carved minstrels' gallery. Its back
wall is Elizabethan plaster and half-timber work.

***Hand painted tile picture over the dining room
fireplace was specially made for Charlford.***

The dining room is more intimate than the drawing room with a
vaulted plaster ceiling incorporating Tudor rose designs. Walls are
plaster, and the doorways are outlined in stone. The fireplace has blue
and white tiles which were selected personally by Johnson.

The library, its ceiling crossed with rough-hewn beams, opens off the
drawing room, and nearby is the Rocky Mountain Room, which is small
and inviting, set in a tower, with a panoramic view of the mountains.
In addition, there are two bedroom suites on the first floor.

Floors in the drawing room are pegged random strips of wood. There
is a honeycomb tile floor in the dining room, and square tiles have been
set in the floor in the gallery. The Rocky Mountain Room has a stone
floor.

The second floor of the original Scottish castle would have been the battlement with watch towers reached by steep, narrow, curved staircases. At Charlford, the towers were turned into bedrooms and a narrow walkway along the battlement enclosed to form a passageway. The high tower above the Rocky Mountain Room has been made into a tiny library. Above it is a battlement, which is a wonderful spot to watch the sun set behind the Front Range.

Surrounding the castle are various utilitarian buildings constructed of the same volcanic stone and sedimentary rock. The garage has an incongruously flat roof, the result of a contractor's misreading of the architect's specifications. As a result the garage roof was higher than that of the house, and Johnson ordered it sliced off.

Johnson and his wife lived in Charlford with intermittent stays in their Denver town house until 1949. The castle stood vacant for five years until it was purchased by a family who renamed it Cherokee Ranch. Like the Cherokee Indians, the new owners had migrated west from Tennessee and thought the name appropriate.

They named not only the ranch but various sections of it as well. The twisting trail that cuts across the mountain from the highway is called Rattlesnake Road. And when they enlarged the property to 6,200 acres to include the mountain Johnson originally picked for the site of the castle, they named the peak Cherokee Mountain.

Built as a vacation home, Charlford, now Cherokee Ranch, has been turned into a working ranch where its owner breeds prize-winning Santa Gertrudis cattle. The castle, unlike many of Colorado's historic homes which have been frozen in time by historic restoration, retains the eclectic air sought by Burnham Hoyt. It is a castle that has telescoped the changes of 500 years but continues to change to meet its owner's needs.

Bibliography

Bancroft, Caroline. *Famous Aspen.* Boulder: Johnson Publishing Co., 1951.

Bancroft, Caroline. *Unique Ghost Towns and Mountain Spots.* Boulder: Johnson Publishing Co., 1961.

Blair, Edward. *Leadville: Colorado's Magic City.* Boulder: Pruett Publishing Co., 1980.

Byers, William N. *Encyclopedia of Biography of Colorado.* Chicago: Century Publishing and Engraving Co., 1901.

Crofutt, George A. *Croffutt's Grip-Sack Guide of Colorado,* 1885 edition. Boulder: Johnson Books, 1981.

Eberhart, Perry. *Guide to the Colorado Ghost Towns and Mining Camps.* Athens Ohio: Swallow Press, 1984.

Fiester, Mark. *Blasted Beloved Breckenridge.* Boulder: Pruett Publishing Co., 1973.

Fort Collins Junior Woman's Club. *The Avery House Collection.* Fort Collins, 1976.

Gilliland, Mary Ellen. *Summit.* Silverthorne: Alpenrose Press, 1980.

Gregory, Doris H. *A Walk Into History.* Long Beach: Cascade Publications, 1982.

Gregory, Doris H. *Wheeler Family of Ouray 1876–1942.* Unpublished manuscript, 1982.

Griswold, Don and Jean. *A Carbonate Camp Called Leadville.* Denver: University of Denver Press, 1951.

Hall, Frank. *History of the State of Colorado,* Vols. 1–4. Chicago: The Blakely Printing Co., 1889.

Hollenback, Frank R. *Central City and Black Hawk, Colorado: Then and Now.* Denver: Sage Books, 1961.

Lee, Mabel Barbee. *Cripple Creek Days.* Garden City: Doubleday & Co., 1958.

Maass, John. *The Gingerbread Age.* New York: Bramhall House, 1957.

McLean, Evalyn Walsh. *Father Struck It Rich.* Boston: Little, Brown and Co., 1936.

Pritchett, Lulita Crawford. *Maggie By My Side.* Steamboat Springs: The Steamboat Pilot, 1976.

Pritchett, Lulita Crawford. *The Cabin at Medicine Springs.* New York: Franklin Watts Inc., 1958.

Progressive Men of Western Colorado. Chicago: A. W. Bowen & Co., 1905.

Ruland, Sylvia. *The Lion of Redstone.* Boulder: Johnson Books, 1981.

Sprague, Marshall. *Massacre: The Tragedy at White River.* Lincoln: University of Nebraska Press, 1980.

Sprague, Marshall. *Money Mountain.* Boston: Little, Brown and Co., 1953.

Stone, Wilbur Fisk. *History of Colorado,* Vols. 1–4. Chicago: S. J. Clarke Publishing Co., 1918.

Swanson, Evadene Burris. *Fort Collins Yesterdays.* Fort Collins, 1975.

Tarkington, Booth. *The Magnificent Ambersons.* New York: Doubleday & Co., 1918.

Vandenbusche, Duane. *The Gunnison Country.* Gunnison: B&B Printers. 1980.

Wolle, Muriel Sibell. *Stampede to Timberline.* Athens Ohio: Swallow Press, 1949.

Wolle, Muriel Sibell. *Timberline Tailings.* Athens Ohio: Swallow Press, 1977.

Wood, Myron and Nancy. *Central City: A Ballad of the West.* Colorado Springs: Chaparral Press, 1963.

NEWSPAPERS AND PERIODICALS

The Colorado Magazine

Colorado Prospector

Denver Post

Evening Chronicle (Leadville)

Greeley Tribune

Lake City Mining Register

Leadville Weekly Democrat

Rocky Mountain News

Salida Daily Mountain Mail

The Silver World

Solid Muldoon

The Western Architect and Building News

The Western Grocer, Butcher and Clerk

Western Slope Prospector